# *Sunset*

# *Landscaping for Western Living*

*By the Editors of Sunset Magazine and Sunset Books*

Lane Books · Menlo Park, California

# Foreword

What are your landscape needs? Perhaps you just moved into a new home with a bare lot and you will have to start from scratch. Or you may own an older home with plenty of overgrown shrubbery and little in the way of outdoor livability. Whatever your situation happens to be, the pages that follow should help you not only to define your needs but to fulfill them.

This book differs from most other landscaping books in one fundamental way: It was written and edited especially for Western home owners. Most of the photographs and how-to-do-it information have been published in recent issues of *Sunset*, The Magazine of Western Living. Additionally, on pages 16 to 27 you will find a collection of some of the favorite garden schemes of contemporary Western landscape architects.

Whether you want to remodel for outdoor living space, or put in a streetside garden, or add a deck, or landscape a children's play area, or select the most reliable plants for your garden's basic framework, you will find a wealth of ideas in this book. Rather than copy any one landscape plan to the letter, try to combine features of several of them with thoughts of your own; then, not only will you come up with a scheme that is distinctly yours, but you very likely will develop a keen appreciation of the creative opportunities that make landscaping in the West unique and enjoyable.

Second Printing June 1968

# Contents

# The Western Approach to Home Landscaping

It was back in the 1930's that the outdoor barbecue first captured the fancy of the Westerner. In doing so, it changed the course of landscaping. Suburban home owners went out-of-doors to cook and entertain, and, in most cases, they found the garden or back yard was not designed for that use. There was no privacy, and sometimes the next-door neighbors were embarrassed; tables and chairs poked holes in the lawn; often the sun was too hot, the wind too strong, the evenings too chilly.

Obviously, before outdoor space could be used, it had to be made more habitable. If much the same kind of living was to take place outdoors as indoors, the same problems had to be solved—garden furniture arrangement, hallways (pathways) for circulation, a floor (paving) for tables and chairs, walls (fences, hedges) for privacy, even heating and cooling for personal comfort.

Suddenly, a set of factors seldom dealt with in conventional landscaping became important. Sun and wind control, and areas for dining, entertaining, playing, and working became first considerations in the Western landscape approach. And the Western home owner built "barbecue shelters," "wind controls," "garden rooms," "overheads."

These experiment-minded Westerners presented a fertile field to the landscape architect who understood them. What they were willing to take, the architects were more than willing to give, and a new type of landscape architecture began to flourish in the West. It was a new type, at least, to the home owner who felt no immediate need to decorate his grounds with plants but was excited about "fixing up the place" to get more living out of it.

He could understand the very practical purpose of landscaping for use. He happily applied the word landscaping to paving a patio, planting a wind or sun screen, building a deck, or roofing over a garden corner to create an "outdoor room." Landscaping, in short, summed up all the things he did to make hours in the garden more livable. The important change was that thousands of families accepted landscaping in this new sense as a natural and normal development in modern living.

This new kind of landscaping has not evolved as a style. It has grown out of the belief that landscaping is for people in search of new experiences in living. Call it site planning, or land use, or landscaping; it is planning the garden for use by people.

Because people are its reference points, this new Western landscaping is quite universal in its application. Wherever it occurs—in Seattle or Los Angeles, in Phoenix or Boise—it involves the same guiding principles of weather control and adaptability to people's needs and desires: to accept or reject gardening; to be absorbed in the arrangement of flowers, shrubs, and trees, or to just sit in the shade; to enjoy close communion with plants, or people; to create a garden picture from a kitchen window or to borrow space from a garden by extending the living room into it.

In this book we have brought together the work of many Western landscape architects. Practically every attitude toward landscaping is in evidence. Every major Western climate is represented—from the frost free winters of the coastal strip to the zero winters east of the Cascades and in the intermountain area; from the mild and moist springtimes of the Northwest coast to the dry, sun-blasted summers of the interior deserts. It is not surprising to find great differences in attitudes and techniques in a collection of many gardens in many climates. But it is both surprising and significant to find that underneath the apparent differences there is a basic approach, common to all.

*FROM STUDY-LIBRARY one looks out on patio shaded by a white alder (Alnus rhombifolia). Stream-washed rocks, liriopes cover ground. Design: Kathryn Stedman.*

*FENCES can be delicate screens of various designs that complement foliage and glorify colors of the garden. This garden is in the Pacific Northwest, and shows such a combination. A piece of simple sculpture provides the accent and focal point. The design is by Eckbo, Royston, and Williams.*

The landscaping we call Western landscaping is based on these fundamentals:

*Western landscaping's first concern is people—their activities and their comfort in the garden.*

*Western landscaping is concerned with beauty—giving people pleasant sensory and emotional experiences.*

*Western landscaping is concerned with experimentation in design—new uses for old standbys, new strains, shrubs used as trees, trees used as shrubs, and a truly limitless list of "for instances."*

The measuring stick of Western landscape design is people—men, women, and children in pursuit of ways to satisfy their varying interests out of doors.

People: Their height measures fences, shrubs, trees, and all vertical and overhead elements.

People: Their line of vision determines whether a fence will provide privacy or merely separation.

People: Their relationship to a tree determines the kind of tree to be planted . . . Shade trees to walk under . . . Trees to look upon . . . Trees for privacy.

People: Their relationship to shrubs determines the best height for a particular planting. Ankle-high to cover the ground; knee-high for direction; waist-high for traffic control, partial enclosure; chest-high for division of space; above eye level for protective enclosure.

People: Their height and line of vision measure garden space as small and cramped or large and expansive.

People in motion outdoors require more space than they do when moving through the house. Two people can walk side by side on a 4-foot garden path, but a 5-foot width gives them freedom to stroll and raise their eyes from the path. The width of a wheel-barrow measured from knuckle to knuckle, the width of a clothes basket from elbow to elbow—these measurements determine the width of gates, passageways, and other openings.

A child on wheels establishes the dimensions of paved play areas. A tricycle can stay on a 24-inch walk, turn in a 4-foot circle. But three or four children on wheels need space for action.

Patios without furniture and without people may look like bare, cold spaces in need of planting. But people, more colorful than shrubs, are dominant elements in the picture when the garden is in use. Outdoors as well as indoors, people need room for their clutter, leftovers, accumulations, whimsy. And when it is time to tidy up, they need outdoor storage places. The space people need for loafing, conversing, eating, should determine the size of the terrace or patio.

However, sun and wind controls, play space, and work space do not make a complete garden. *Landscape design is concerned with beauty—giving people pleasant sensory and emotional experiences.* Satisfying physical needs is not enough. How a human being reacts to his surroundings is equally important. Will he be excited by movement in the garden, intrigued by variety, soothed by quiet, stimulated by color, kept interested by change?

A beautiful garden harbors secrets and surprises. It is never completely discovered. It contains sentimental values which change with the growth and age of the garden. There are more depths and dimensions of beauty in the garden to be lived in than in the garden to be just looked at. All the senses are involved. You react to what you touch, smell, hear, as well as what you see. We are talking about gardens such as those shown on the following pages.

CENTRAL PATIO *is viewed through frame provided by large glass window. Bird-of-paradise appears in foreground; ferns and potted citrus are contained within patio. Looking through the glass doors at the end of the patio, you can see an arbor beyond. The design is by Edward Williams.*

SHRINE *of stone and water located in Utah's high country. Gardens such as this are places to nurture memories. Dainty star flower, Mahonia repens, fringes rocks over pool. Water birch and smooth sumac cast reflections in calm surface. The stone, much in evidence, is softened by plants. Design: Leon Frehner.*

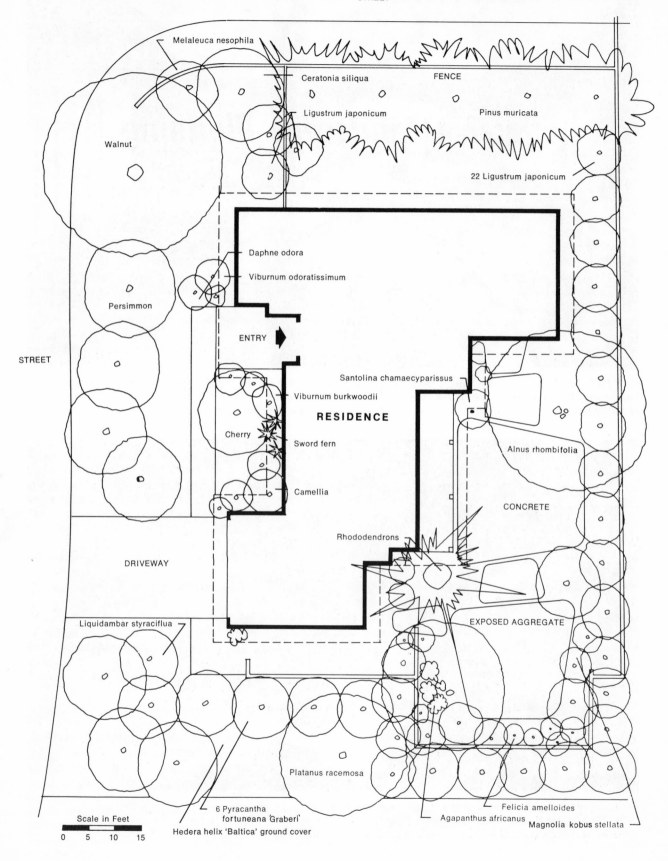

STREET

Melaleuca nesophila

Ceratonia siliqua

FENCE

Ligustrum japonicum

Pinus muricata

Walnut

22 Ligustrum japonicum

Daphne odora

Viburnum odoratissimum

Persimmon

STREET

ENTRY

Santolina chamaecyparissus

Viburnum burkwoodii

RESIDENCE

Cherry

Sword fern

Alnus rhombifolia

Camellia

CONCRETE

Rhododendrons

DRIVEWAY

Liquidambar styraciflua

EXPOSED AGGREGATE

Platanus racemosa

Felicia amelloides

Scale in Feet

6 Pyracantha
fortuneana 'Graberi'

Agapanthus africanus

Magnolia kobus stellata

0   5   10   15

Hedera helix 'Baltica' ground cover

# Effective Landscape Planning

To make the most of your particular plot of land requires planning. Whether you are starting with a new house that is not landscaped or remodeling an older garden, you can best proceed by taking stock of what you have. Items to check and directions for putting tentative plans and ideas on paper are included in this chapter.

A feature of this chapter is the collection of plan sketches that show how some of our leading Western landscape architects have imaginatively dealt with different shaped lots—square, narrow, deep, pie-shaped, corner. Another chapter highlight is the section on ways to control your garden's climate (control wind and sun and you control the livability of your garden).

## TAKE INVENTORY OF YOUR SITE

"Take inventory" may be too strong a term—too serious sounding—for the process of getting ready to landscape. To put it another way, look at what you have before you plan what you would like. Since this type of landscaping began because people wanted to do more everyday living out of doors, we will start with the most important factor that will hinder or help you—your climate. How do the sun and the wind affect your property?

### The sun — its assets & liabilities

The path of the sun, the amount of sun, and its intensity through the seasons of the year and the hours

of the day, affect the location, kind, and amount of your outdoor living areas, and determine the kind of plants you can grow. If the number of warm sunny days is limited, you naturally seek to develop areas where the sun can be trapped. You appreciate paved areas of concrete, brick, and asphalt that absorb the heat of the sun and re-radiate it to increase temperatures near their surfaces.

Paving that is shaded in summer but exposed to the sun in the winter (as it is under a deciduous tree) is ideal. Where sun and rain alternate many days in the year, glass or fiberglass overheads multiply your outdoor hours.

Where the amount of sun is limited, look to south walls to reflect extra heat for those plants that need it; avoid plantings that will shut off the sun in the fall, winter, and spring months. If summer temperatures are high, you not only attempt to avoid the sun by creating overhead screens of foliage or structure, but you also put in a minimum of paving that cannot be shaded. Of course, the time of day you plan to use the garden will also influence what you do about the sun. Pavements too hot for afternoon use may be just the thing to take the chill out of the after-sundown air.

In western North America, the sun is never directly overhead, although we may mistakenly think of it that way. This means that a tree or overhead structure will never cast all of its shade directly beneath it.

At midday, the sun is always somewhere to the south of a point directly overhead; at sunrise it's always somewhere between the northeast and southeast points on your horizon; and at sunset it's between the northwest and southwest points on the other horizon.

How high the sun may be within this area at any particular time of day depends on the time of the year. The sun's arc is low in winter, high in summer (but never high enough to be overhead at noon).

*CORNER LOT exposes two sides to public, requires screening for privacy. Problem solved by fences, plants. Landscape architect: John Carmack, San Francisco.*

To a small degree the sun's angle on any day also depends on how far north of the equator you live. But this, the effect of latitude, makes only a comparatively minor change in sun angles between the Mexican and Canadian borders.

### The wind — cooling or chilling?

Whether it's cool, dry, hot, or moist, a wind or breeze can change outdoor comfort for better or worse as drastically as changes in temperature. How can you take inventory of the wind before you have lived in a place for a year? One source of information is your neighbors; you can share their experience. The "lean" of trees in the neighborhood will tell the story of prevailing winds. But the direction of the prevailing wind around your house may not be the same as it is around the house next door. Wind flows like water —spilling over obstacles, breaking into several currents, eddying and twisting.

No one experiences exactly the same temperature as the thermometer at the weather bureau. When the weather bureau says that the temperature is 68°, it means to say that a thermometer *in the shade, protected from the wind, reads 68°*. If there is a 10 to 15-mile-an-hour breeze, a person in the shade in the breeze may feel that the temperature is about 62°. If the breeze is stopped and the patio is in sunlight, the person will feel a comfortable 75-78°.

Of course, the cooling effect of a breeze becomes an advantage when summer temperatures are above 90°. In such cases, the path of the prevailing summer wind is an important design factor. You won't want to block the wind with obstacles like shrub plantings and solid fences. You may prefer vertical louvers to literally "catch a breeze."

In checking the wind problem around your house, remember that the house itself is your biggest windbreak but may need additions to be effective. In some cases, the wind spills over the house and drops on the patio. Remember, too, that a solid barrier is not always the most efficient. Wind washes over solid fence as a stream of water would wash over a solid barrier. At about the distance equal to fence height, protection drops rapidly. You feel 1.8° warmer 12 feet away than in the unprotected area.

For the fence with vertical laths spaced about ½ inch apart, the lowest reading is close to the fence, the highest, 12 feet away. At 12 feet you would feel 7° warmer than when standing on windward side of the fence.

A 45° baffle into wind gives greater protection close to the fence than any control tested. Beyond the maximum 7.5° increase, comfort drop is gradual, extending effective protection to distance equal to over twice fence height.

### The seasons

The opportunities for outdoor living are, of course, fewer in severe climates than in mild climates. But there are two ways to count your opportunities. You can estimate how few days there are, or how many. To the pessimist, 60 days or 120 half days of outdoor living weather is a fraction of 365; to the optimist, those 60 days add up to a total that is four times as long as his vacation.

If you base your decision for landscaping for garden use on the proportion of completely comfortable rainless days to the total of wet or chilly days, you wouldn't do much in any short summer season climate—or anywhere. Completely comfortable outdoor living, hour after hour and day after day, is very rare. But each step you take to modify the climate increases the use of the outdoors.

If you pave an area immediately adjacent to the house, that area can be used between showers when the lawn would be too wet. Stop the breeze that sweeps across the terrace, and you can enjoy it in sunlight when air temperatures are much lower than the accepted 78° comfort temperature.

Put glass or fiberglass over head, and many rainy days become pleasant. (The Northwest, with its days of warm rain, might find an adaptation of Hawaii's lanai a good idea. The lanai takes care of many tropical showers.) When you take inventory of your climate, note the number of days that might be pleasant in the garden if you did something about them.

### Your piece of land

What is the shape of your lot? How will its form affect your landscaping? Each lot shape has its advantages and disadvantages.

*The inside rectangular lot* sets up a rigid rectangle of clearly defined space. The view of neighboring roofs and windows must come into your planning. Your back garden may be influenced by as many as five neighboring families. If, by some miracle, all five could get together on a program of tall shrub and tree planting, the problems of getting privacy and of sun and wind protection could be worked out more efficiently and at less expense than if each home owner goes his own way.

*The long narrow lot* has many advantages. You can easily zone it into areas by use—outdoor room, children's play area, work center, etc. The difficulty of getting these various areas to flow together as one garden is the design trick you'll have to solve. There are several examples throughout the book.

*The pie-shaped lot*, with the narrow end toward the street, is probably the most desirable of all. It gives least space on the street and most space behind the house.

*The corner lot* presents a difficult problem when you are trying for maximum private space. Compared to an interior lot where you give up the setback space on the front only, the corner lot makes you give up both side and front to the public. In the corner lot you lose private space, but you get a feeling of openness that you can't have in the more boxed-in interior lot.

## Soil, drainage

In a small garden, you needn't worry about a lack of plant food, or whether the soil is sand or clay. You can improve poor soils with chemical soil conditioners and quantities of organic matter such as peat moss.

But if your soil is shallow and underlaid with a compacted layer that is impervious to water and roots, or if water does not drain from your lot, you must either correct the situation or plant as if you had no soil. For example, plant above the ground in raised beds.

## Indoor-outdoor relationship

The development of outdoor space for living can give the interior rooms an entirely new dimension. Check to see possible garden views from the windows of the house. Can the patio be built so that it is visually an extension of the living room? Would a kitchen patio be more usable? If indoor floor level is above ground level, are the steps from house to garden easy to negotiate? Would a deck at floor level make the living room larger and entrance into the garden easier?

## Utility connections

Will sewer pipes or a septic tank drain field interfere with tree plantings? Are water outlets placed so that future use is possible without cutting through lawns or pavement? Should there be a water faucet in the garden work center? A drain? What connections are there for sprinkler systems? If you plan to light the garden at night, do you have outdoor electric outlets?

## You and your family

It's much safer to plan a garden to fit the natural habits of your family than to aim at changing those habits after your garden is built. If you are careless

housekeepers, the garden shouldn't require you to be neat. If the children are rough-housers and are allowed free run indoors, don't plan a garden that can't take punishment. A good garden is like a good house—it should accommodate the people who live in it and adapt to their changing interests and changing needs. How distant in the future are teen-age parties? Grandchildren?

*What kind of a gardener are you?* Do you garden because you must, or is gardening still a new experience for you? If you are an experienced gardener and love it, can you expect to be with the garden every week that it needs you, or will you be called away on long trips? Will a sprinkler system, installed the first thing, make routine maintenance easier?

*What kind of workmen in your family?* Can you put together simple structures with hammer and saw? Does the prospect of mixing concrete intimidate you? How much work do you get from your teen-agers? Is the hard work of building, digging, paving, and planting your family's idea of fun?

*Can you go fast or must you go slow?* Two things are involved here: one is your budget, the other is the leisure time you can devote to installing your garden. For many home owners working on their own, a reasonable garden-installation timetable is two to four years. Do you tend to over-estimate your ability to carry through a project?

## Space requirements

**Patio area.** If this book does nothing else for you except to increase the size of your garden living room, it will pay its way. Whether the patio will be used for entertaining, or play, or just sitting, it is always more satisfying when over-sized.

**Play areas.** Are your children preschool age? They will want sand and water and tricycle runs now, but you will probably want to convert this area to another purpose within a few years.

**Game areas.** Garden games are fun; they also swallow up space. Will you want a basketball hoop now or later? Can you use the front driveway for this and other games? Will you want space for badminton, croquet, tetherball, shuffleboard?

**Outdoor work area.** In many parts of the West, the weather is pleasant enough for you to do woodworking, painting, cabinet making, and many other craft and hobby projects outdoors. Teen-agers like to tinker with an old car. Small boys need to build things. You may want to plan space for these outdoor activities. Don't forget to include an area for your clothes line where it will be convenient to the utility area, but removed visually.

**Outdoor storage area.** A minimum amount of outdoor storage is essential for garden tools, lawn mower, garden cart or wheelbarrow, paints, garden chemicals, peat moss, fertilizers, ladder, lawn furniture. And where will you store firewood and lumber? If you have no basement or attic, you may want a garden storage structure.

**Trash area.** Most families tend to accumulate bulky trash. It's a good idea to have a place out of sight where you can hide this accumulation between burnings or trips to the city dump.

**Plant shelters.** If you're a serious gardener, or if you become one in time, you may want a garden work center, a lathhouse, a greenhouse. How big should it be? Where will it go?

**Food garden.** You may want to grow some of your own vegetables. You may want a small family orchard. Very often a garden can provide both vegetables and fruit without sacrificing beauty or play space, but you must allow for them in your plan.

**Water.** The sound and sight of water are always pleasant in a garden. You may want a small fountain, a small pool, or a swimming pool. The fountain or small pool is easy, but a 16 by 28-foot swimming pool and the paving around it require a minimum of about 850 square feet.

## PUT YOUR PLAN ON PAPER

Your first practical step in getting your design on paper is to make a "scale" drawing of your lot—draw a plot plan.

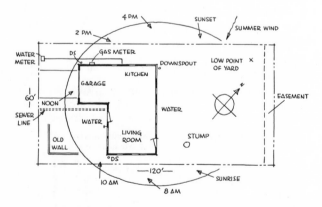

### Draw a plot plan of your lot

The purpose of your plot plan is to show in measured relationship the limiting factors discussed in the previous section. You'll save yourself many hours of measuring if you can locate any of the following:

1. *Deed map.* Shows actual dimensions and orientations of your property. If you do not have this, you might get information at the city hall, county courthouse, title company, bank, or mortgage company.

2. *Contour map.* For hill sites this is very important, and it is now sometimes required by law prior to issuing a building permit. Made by an engineer, it shows 1-foot, 2-foot, 5-foot, or 10-foot contours—in other words, it shows the exact *shape* of your site. It sometimes also indicates property dimensions, streets, sidewalks, utilities, large trees, rocks, etc.

3. *Architect's drawings or house plans.* Should show site plan, floor plan, elevations, how related to site, windows, doors, roof, utilities, hose bib connections, downspouts, footing details. NOTE: Check with builder or architect, or check personally, to see whether any later changes have been made. Often homes are shifted on the lot several feet one way or another to utilize the site better.

Make a large map on graph paper (24 by 36 inches) that will show in clear detail just exactly what you have to work with. Draw to the largest scale the paper will allow—generally, ¼-inch equaling 1 foot. This will be your base map. Slipping this base map under the top sheet on a pad of tracing paper, you can later sketch out designs to your heart's content. (You can buy graph paper and a pad of large-sized tracing paper at a stationery store.)

Bring out the check list you have made up from your inventory and place it alongside this basic plot plan. You now have in front of you all of the physical restrictions and requirements imposed by your lot, and a list of all your needs. You are ready to go ahead with your planning.

Lay a sheet of tracing paper over the base map on which you have outlined house and lot. All the work of getting the house and lot on the graph paper is safe from being messed up. If you make a false move, nothing is lost except one piece of tracing paper. You can swing that pencil with abandon.

So now you sit looking down at a piece of paper, and your head is filled with 15 or 20 items which must be arranged on that paper. Don't feel that this design-on-paper idea is a silly crutch for beginners. As you work out any garden, you are forced to make dozens of decisions. And unless those decisions are recorded, they will be lost. A plan is a record of decisions and a constant check on the accuracy of the decisions. No expert planner relies on his memory. Nor does he make off-the-cuff decisions. It costs money to change a line fixed in cement, but it costs nothing to erase it on paper.

But you are still looking at that piece of tissue paper. Afraid to begin?

## Start your plan with "doodles"

If you're afraid to start your design plan, try "doodling." Many landscape architects work from doodles —miniature patterns that set the theme of the design. "If it doesn't look interesting in a doodle, it won't look good when it's built." Doodles are helpful to many amateurs because by over-simplification they rule out minor details that get in the way of the basic plan. Most important, they do not have the serious aspect of a full-sized landscape plan. They are experiments in approach. They allow comparisons.

Doodles come quickly. You can doodle a dozen plans in miniature while you are getting ready to put one final plan on paper. Just remember that the shape of your doodle plan should be in proportion to your lot. Of the principles that have been advanced in the previous chapter, this is the most important:

*Design is for people—for their activities and comfort in the garden.*

You will be on your way to a usable garden if you follow this principle by providing adequate patio and play space; by blocking the hot summer sun (but inviting the warming winter sun); by deflecting the disagreeable wind (or sometimes catching a refreshing or cooling breeze).

Since the sun and wind will, in general, control the placement of the major elements in your garden, you may find yourself placing these elements in such a pleasant relationship that no thought of design as such is necessary.

If they do not arrange themselves so easily, consider these main points:

1. *To avoid confusion, to get simplicity and order in your design, plan with the recognizable shapes of the square, the rectangle, and the circle.*

2. *In the small garden with fixed limits, create the illusion of greater space by not allowing the eye to measure the complete space at a glance.*

In working out your own design, you should be aware of the special devices used by the leading landscape architects. The photographs of their work say over and over again:

1. *Design generously, then count costs.*

To get a feeling of luxury in the garden (and where else can it be bought so cheaply?) you need only take a step here and there beyond necessity. A 10 by 16-foot patio seems more than adequate to most builders; but a 12 by 30-foot patio, part concrete, part ground cover, part gravel, is a very luxurious thing.

In most builders' houses, the usual step between the house and the patio is only as wide as the door. Lengthen it and widen it and you not only go in and out of the house with ease, but you have a garden seat as well.

2. *Design boldly so that later plant growth will not completely erase your design.*

Design should make a strong and definite statement. Unless you lead from strength, growing plants will erase the design almost as soon as it is executed. What may appear too strong the first year is gentled and quieted by plant growth in the third year. The low wall, the wide mowing strip, the raised bed, are strong, built-in, permanent lines used boldly by the landscape designer.

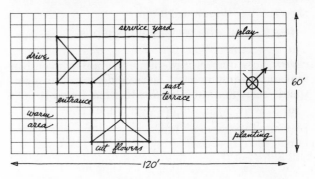

USE TRACING PAPER to indicate the areas that you will need. Show sun and wind protection where needed. When you remove the paper it may look like this.

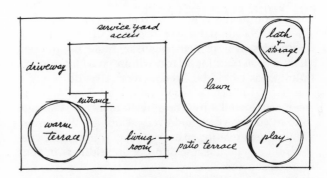

EXPERIMENT with the relationships of space and plane, form and line, until the design suits you. The circle is suggested so continue to use it as a basic theme.

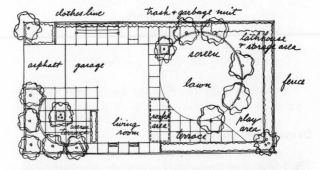

ENTRANCE AREAS, the patio, and the paved surfaces come next. Following the lines of the house, the patio becomes a rectangle. Paths control foot traffic.

3. *Design can direct the steps of people, spread them out through the garden, bring them together, draw them to an entrance or an exit.*

For example, if the patio floor appears to be a part of the house, the edge of the patio will set the limit for movement of most people. However, if a wide path flows from the patio to another paved area in the garden—under a tree, perhaps—people will spread out through the garden. A second sitting area at a distance from the house gives everyone visual permission to move into the garden.

## How to plan with rectangular shapes

Now, take an entirely different approach; and instead of using the circle as a guide, take the square and rectangle. Many an amateur has found it helpful to work with a uniform "module" (i.e., a unit of space, repeated again and again, like squares on a checkerboard or bricks in a wall). Your module might be 3 by 4, or 4 by 4, or 4 by 5 feet, or almost any larger rectangle that suits your needs.

Using the rectangular module, we can make everything fall neatly into place. There's no question about what spacings to use or what sizes to establish.

Suppose you decide to use a 4 by 5-foot module. All of your walks would be 4 feet or a generous 5 feet in width. Your patio would divide up into 4 by 5 rectangles. One or more of these might be an open 4 by 5-foot planting island within your patio areas. Plant beds would be 4 feet across. A sandbox might be 8 by 10 feet, a raised bed 4 by 5 or 4 by 10 feet, a tree well 4 by 5 or 8 by 10 feet. Every design line in your garden, and every structural dimension, would be in relation to every other. You would benefit from a general sense of order and tidiness in your garden scheme.

The module system offers other advantages. With the dimensions suggested above, you have only 15, 16, or 20 square feet of paving to worry about at any one time. You can mix and pour your concrete for just one rectangle at a time. You lay one rectangle of bricks before you start another. If you're a little bit off with your brick courses, you get a fresh start with the next rectangle.

Here are some of the ways you can go about selecting a module.

A path or walk that is about 4 feet wide will offer easy passage for a wheelbarrow, a wagon, or a bike. A narrower path seems restricted; a wider path may eat up too much space.

The patio wall of your house may be 24 feet wide. A 4-foot division in your patio paving would make 6 modules exactly fit your wall dimension. If you work with bricks, you will avoid brick cutting if your module is an exact multiple of brick dimensions.

Most professionals urge a module no less than 3 by 3 feet; amateur landscapers say a generous module saves work.

Now take the same problem, the same base map, and work out a design using the module system. As the sketches on this page show, the design so far is reasonably satisfying. We've taken care of all the space requirements. Can we check it? How does it rate on these points:

- Could anything be done more simply and work even better?
- Did we make our design strong enough—bold enough—to hold its effect as plants grow?
- Can we get through the garden and around the house with a wheelbarrow?
- Have we provided adequate sun and wind control?

If it passes these tests, you are ready to give it the further refinements that you will pick up by studying this book.

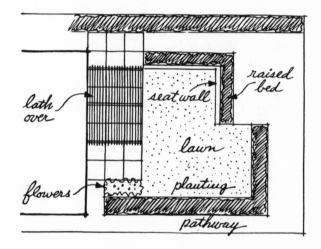

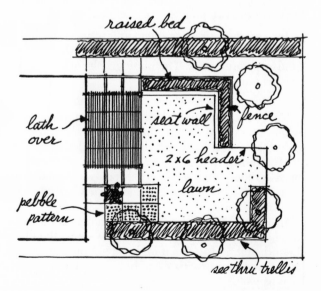

## WHAT SIZE? WHAT SHAPE?

There are no stock plans in landscaping. No two situations are exactly alike. No one plan could be made to exactly fit several situations. But there are great similarities as well as differences. On the preceding pages we accepted the very common rectangular interior lot for our problem. The solutions shown are usable in similar lots. The plans can be successfully copied if the necessary adjustments are made for differences in sun and wind problems.

We now explore the possibilities of adaptable solutions to such sites as the corner lot, the pie-shaped lot, and so on.

First, let's take a look at a typical subdivision lot plan and see how landscape problems differ by types of site. A glance at the map shows that due to the uniform setback from the street, there's a great difference between the amount of streetside or "public" area and private area. In the map below, a 25-foot setback is required.

It's obvious that if you want the largest private garden you'll try for the pie-shaped lots. On the other hand, it is hard to believe that a 10,000-square-foot corner lot will give no more private garden space than a 6,000-square-foot interior lot.

The general rule seems to be that 6-foot fences are allowed only on the secondary street side. A low fence or wall is permitted nearly everywhere, but check local ordinances.

### Long narrow lots

When the long narrow lot is landscaped in the usual pattern of flower and shrub beds on either side and end of a lawn panel, the garden feels like a hallway with a narrow green carpet down the center. The problem is to find ways to give the illusion of width, or at least to prevent the eye from quickly measuring the narrow rectangle.

### Pie-shaped lots

The pie-shaped cul-de-sac lot can give you the greatest proportion of private space to public space of all the lot shapes in a subdivision. The streetside is narrow; the backside, deep.

### Corner lots

Several ways have been used to overcome the unequal proportion between space for public view and space for private use. If you drive around looking for suggestions on how to handle the corner lot, you'll see many solutions that might be denied you. The newer subdivisions are generally more strict in enforcing setbacks. In older residential sections, the problem of privacy was often solved by planting a hedge on the property line next to the sidewalk and letting it grow to 8 feet or more. Some of the later subdivisions allowed a property line fence, 6 feet high, 5 feet from the sidewalk, along one side only.

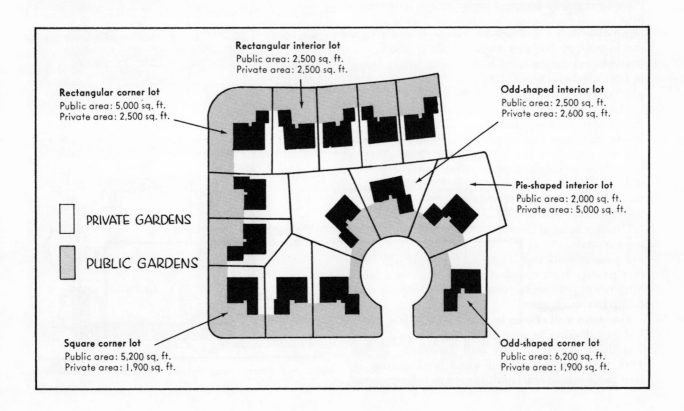

Rectangular interior lot
Public area: 2,500 sq. ft.
Private area: 2,500 sq. ft.

Rectangular corner lot
Public area: 5,000 sq. ft.
Private area: 2,500 sq. ft.

Odd-shaped interior lot
Public area: 2,500 sq. ft.
Private area: 2,600 sq. ft.

Pie-shaped interior lot
Public area: 2,000 sq. ft.
Private area: 5,000 sq. ft.

PRIVATE GARDENS

PUBLIC GARDENS

Square corner lot
Public area: 5,200 sq. ft.
Private area: 1,900 sq. ft.

Odd-shaped corner lot
Public area: 6,200 sq. ft.
Private area: 1,900 sq. ft.

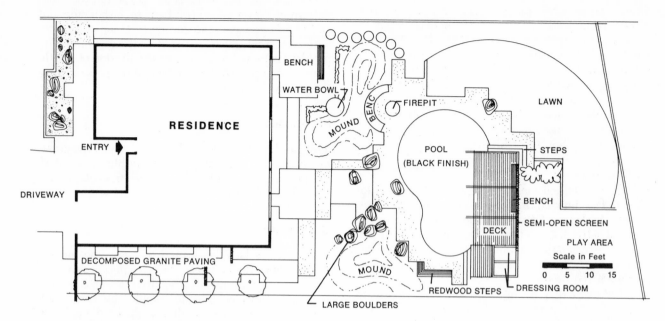

**MAKING THE MOST OF A NARROW LOT** • *Mounds of earth, sweeping curves create the illusion of greater space in this narrow lot. Rocks are combined with plant material in an interesting manner. There is a paved walk along side of the house to the pool area. A play area is contained behind a screen. Landscape architects: Jones/Peterson, Anaheim, California.*

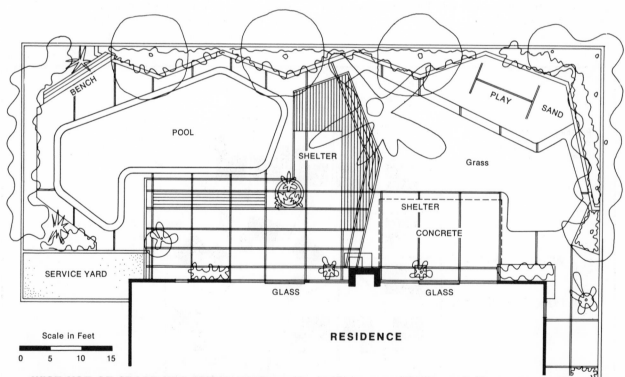

**WISE USE OF SPACE IN A SMALL YARD** • *Narrow lot accommodates a pool, play area for children, and outdoor living area. The pool area is screened off from the remainder of the lot by a fence. Shade is provided by an overhead. Unusual shape of the pool, deck, and screen create the illusion of depth. Landscape architect: Mary Gordon, Palo Alto, California.*

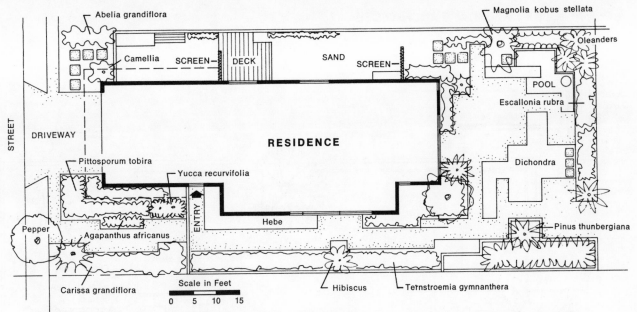

**PLANTING ISLANDS ALTERNATE WITH ACTIVITY AREAS** ● *A series of irregularly shaped concrete areas are alternated with planting islands, deck, and lawn. A pool provides the focal point of interest in one corner of the lot. There are several screens to separate areas of the garden. Large expanses of glass open the house to the garden. Landscape architects: Jones/Peterson, Anaheim, California.*

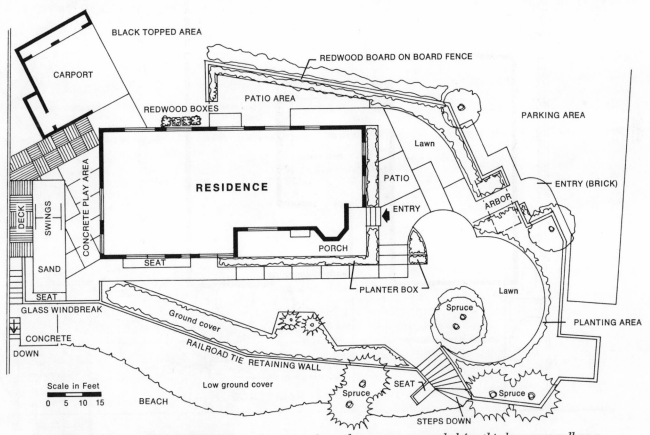

**PRIVACY FOR A BEACH HOUSE** ● *Screening from the street was needed for this house as well as a windbreak. A fence at the edge of the property solved the privacy problem while a glass screen cut the wind flow. A large play area is situated at one end of the house while the adult outdoor area is at the other. Landscape architect: Chandler D. Fairbank, Portland.*

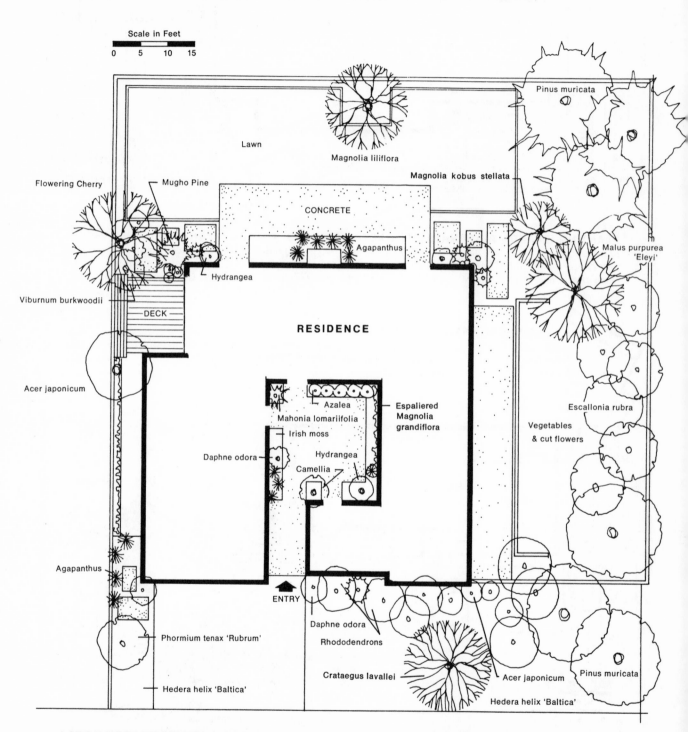

Scale in Feet
0  5  10  15

Pinus muricata

Lawn

Magnolia liliflora

Magnolia kobus stellata

Flowering Cherry

Mugho Pine

CONCRETE

Agapanthus

Malus purpurea 'Eleyi'

Hydrangea

Viburnum burkwoodii

DECK

RESIDENCE

Acer japonicum

Azalea

Espaliered Magnolia grandiflora

Mahonia lomariifolia

Irish moss

Escallonia rubra

Daphne odora

Hydrangea

Vegetables & cut flowers

Camellia

Agapanthus

ENTRY

Daphne odora

Phormium tenax 'Rubrum'

Rhododendrons

Hedera helix 'Baltica'

Crataegus lavallei

Acer japonicum

Pinus muricata

Hedera helix 'Baltica'

**LARGE RESIDENCE WITH GENEROUS OUTDOOR LIVING SPACE** ● *Here is a square lot with the house close to the lot line on one side. Interior court, concrete, deck, and grass areas provide outdoor living space. The planting is concentrated in one major area leaving the remainder of the space for living areas. Landscape architect: John Carmack, San Francisco.*

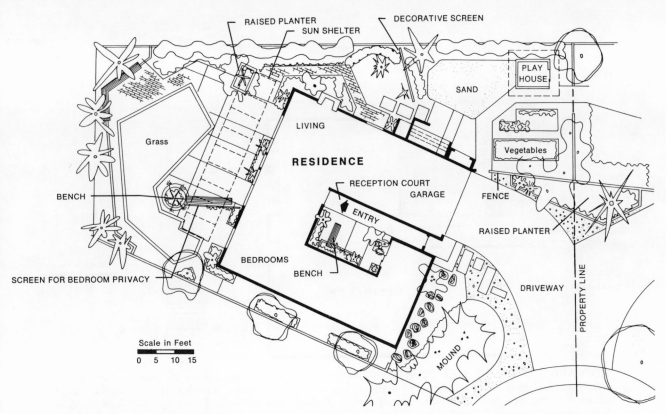

**COOPERATIVE LANDSCAPING ON A CUL-DE-SAC** • *The area on either side of the driveways was planned by the same landscape architect. A play area for children, screened from the street, falls in this area and coordinated planning ties two properties together. Landscape architect: Mary Gordon, Palo Alto, California.*

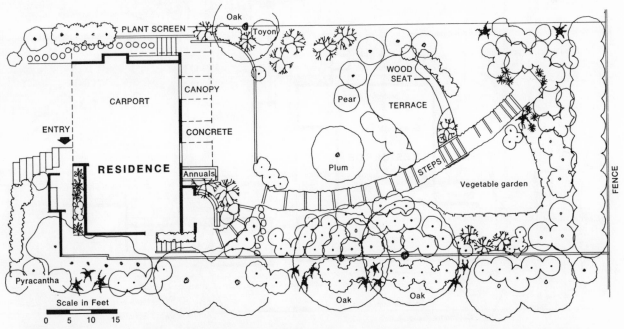

**NARROW LOT . . . STEEP SLOPE . . . OUTDOOR LIVING** • *Redesign of older house and steep, awkward garden. Many of the larger trees were on the property, but much new plant material was added. Slope utilized to create outdoor living and entertaining areas with steps connecting them. Landscape architect: William L. Kapranos, San Rafael, California.*

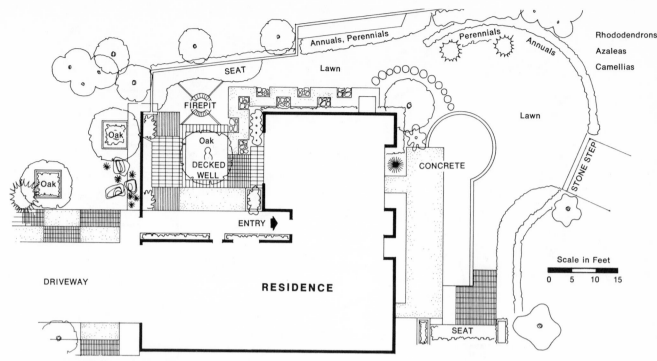

**SIDEYARD, BACKYARD, AND COURTYARD SCHEME** • *Subdivision house with courtyard-living area to be screened from the street and the stepped, higher adjacent garden. Problem was solved by use of plants, building materials. Interesting use of bricks, decking, and concrete. Landscape architect: William L. Kapranos, San Rafael, California.*

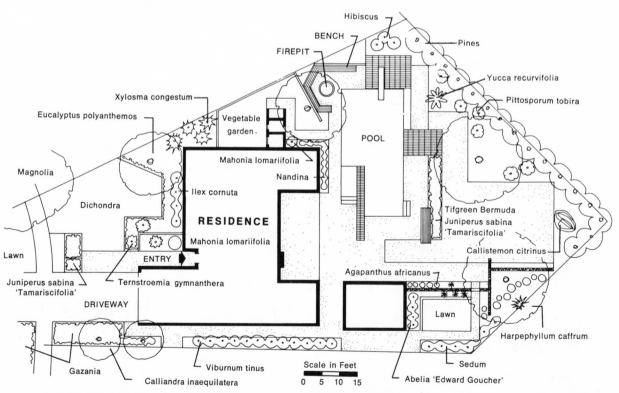

**A SWIMMING POOL IN A GENEROUS SIZED REAR GARDEN** • *The pool occupies a large portion of the garden. Several areas of concrete are alternated with decking, benches. Large paved areas provide outdoor living space. A vegetable garden is tucked away in an enclosed area. The firepit and large bench are located near the pool for ease of entertaining. Landscape architects: Jones/Peterson, Anaheim, Calif.*

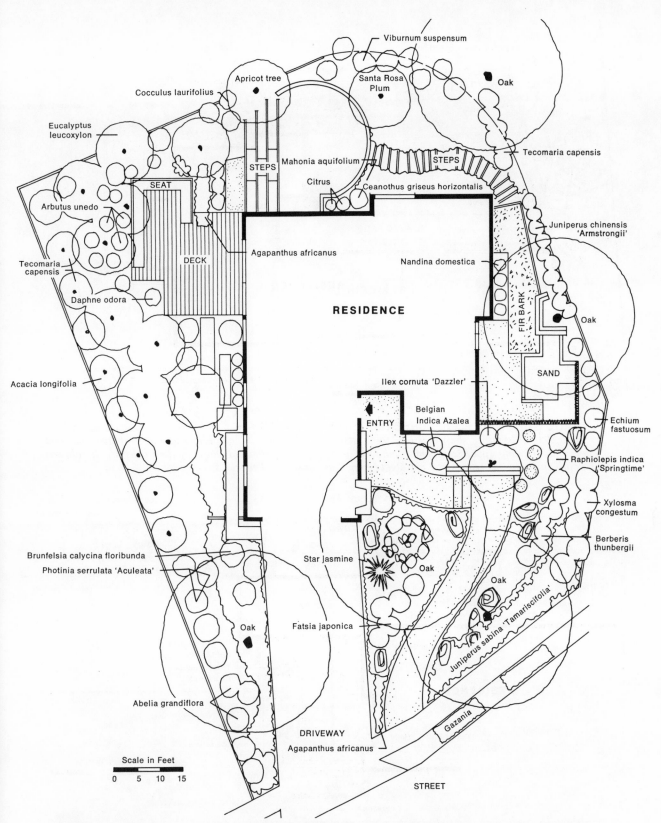

Viburnum suspensum

Apricot tree

Santa Rosa Plum

Oak

Cocculus laurifolius

Eucalyptus leucoxylon

Tecomaria capensis

STEPS

Mahonia aquifolium

STEPS

SEAT

Citrus

Ceanothus griseus horizontalis

Juniperus chinensis 'Armstrongii'

Arbutus unedo

DECK

Agapanthus africanus

Nandina domestica

FIR BARK

Oak

Tecomaria capensis

Daphne odora

RESIDENCE

Acacia longifolia

SAND

Ilex cornuta 'Dazzler'

Belgian Indica Azalea

Echium fastuosum

ENTRY

Raphiolepis indica 'Springtime'

Xylosma congestum

Brunfelsia calycina floribunda

Photinia serrulata 'Aculeata'

Star jasmine

Berberis thunbergii

Oak

Oak

Juniperus sabina 'Tamariscifolia'

Oak

Fatsia japonica

Abelia grandiflora

Gazania

Scale in Feet

0   5   10   15

DRIVEWAY

Agapanthus africanus

STREET

**UNUSUALLY SHAPED LOT WITH SEVERAL OUTDOOR LIVING AREAS** ● *The unusual shape of this lot and the slope provide the opportunity for interesting use of structural elements. Large expanses of glass connect the house with the deck. Several separate outdoor living areas are connected by steps. Landscape architects: Jones/Peterson, Anaheim, California.*

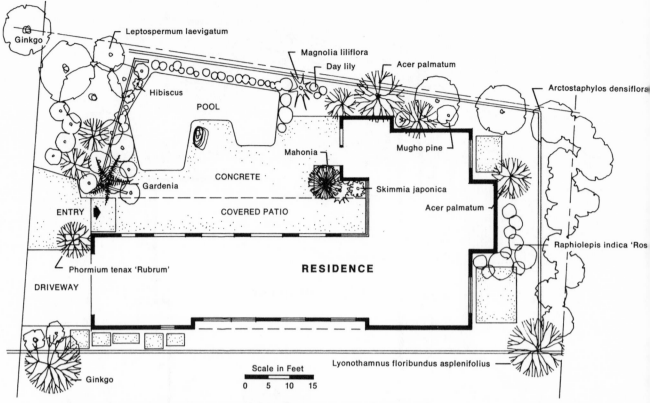

**A LARGE SWIMMING POOL SCREENED FROM NEIGHBORS** • *Long, narrow residence occupies a great deal of this oddly shaped site. Pool is screened off from the neighbors at the property line, and level outdoor living space is provided adjacent to it. Planting, unusual shape of the pool give the illusion of depth to the area. Landscape architect: John Carmack, San Francisco.*

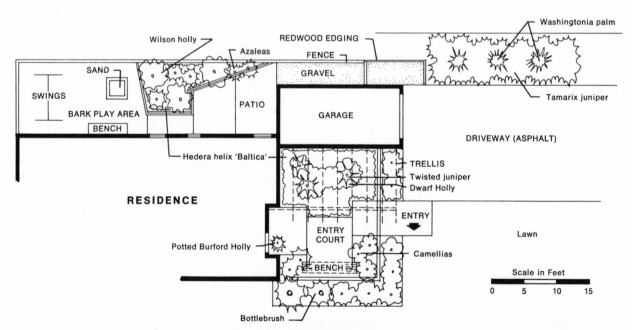

**ENTRY COURT—A GOOD ANSWER FOR A SPACE PROBLEM** • *Narrow lot with very little space for outdoor play or entertaining. A wide range of plant materials are used in the entry court where they can be enjoyed at close hand. The patio is separated from the children's play area by an island of plants. Landscape architect: L. K. Smith, Thousand Oaks, California.*

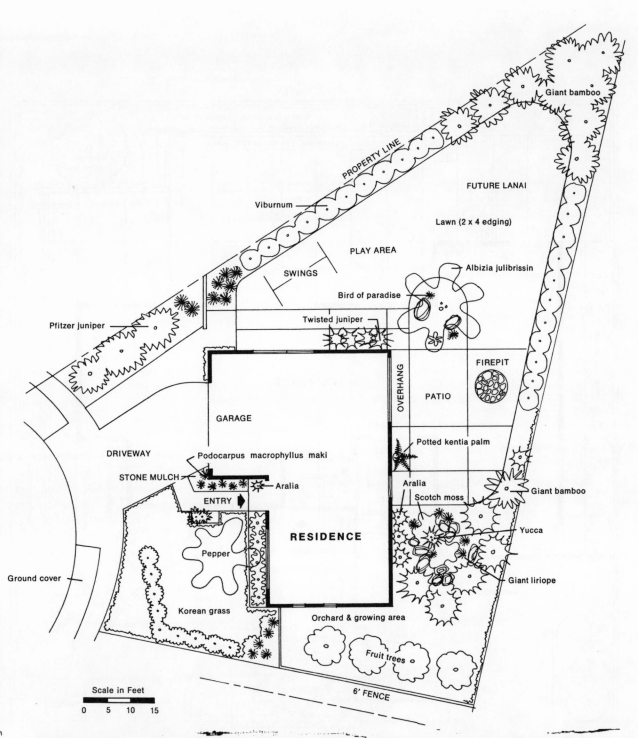

Giant bamboo

PROPERTY LINE

FUTURE LANAI

Viburnum

Lawn (2 x 4 edging)

PLAY AREA

SWINGS

Albizia julibrissin

Bird of paradise

Twisted juniper

Pfitzer juniper

FIREPIT

OVERHANG

PATIO

GARAGE

Potted kentia palm

DRIVEWAY

Podocarpus macrophyllus maki

STONE MULCH

Aralia

ENTRY

Aralia

Scotch moss

Giant bamboo

RESIDENCE

Pepper

Yucca

Ground cover

Giant liriope

Korean grass

Orchard & growing area

Fruit trees

Scale in Feet

0   5   10   15

6' FENCE

**CUL-DE-SAC LOT WITH GENEROUS PRIVATE SPACE** ● *Here is a lot with the narrow end to the street which provides a maximum of private garden space. One end of the property is used as an orchard and growing area and is screened from the neighboring property by a 6-foot fence. The generous paved patio contains a firepit. Landscape architect: L. K. Smith, Thousand Oaks, California.*

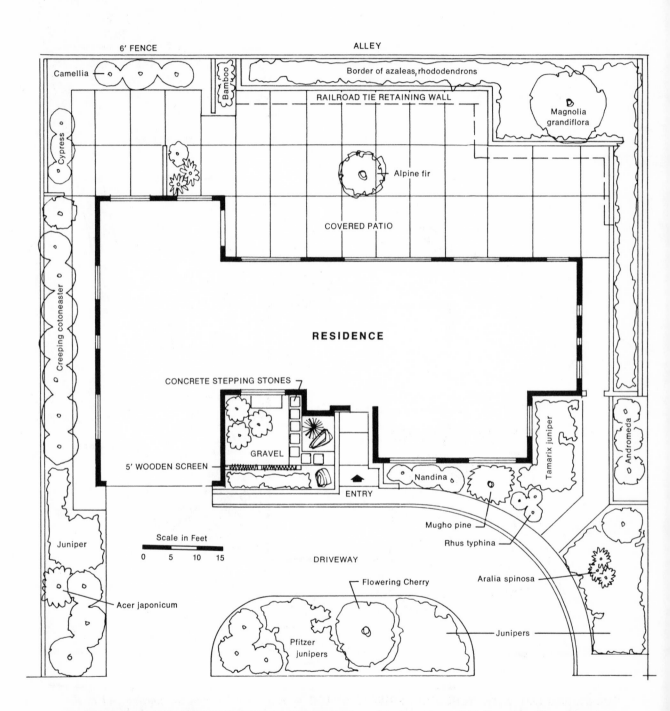

6' FENCE

ALLEY

Camellia

Bamboo

Border of azaleas, rhododendrons

RAILROAD TIE RETAINING WALL

Magnolia grandiflora

Cypress

Alpine fir

COVERED PATIO

Creeping cotoneaster

RESIDENCE

CONCRETE STEPPING STONES

5' WOODEN SCREEN

GRAVEL

Tamarix juniper

Andromeda

Nandina

ENTRY

Mugho pine

Rhus typhina

Juniper

Scale in Feet

0    5    10    15

DRIVEWAY

Aralia spinosa

Acer japonicum

Flowering Cherry

Junipers

Pfitzer junipers

**PLANTING ISLAND FOR A CIRCULAR DRIVEWAY** ● *Privacy is required from the alley that runs in back of this property. A 6-foot fence solves this problem. There is a large paved expanse for outdoor living. A planting island in front of the circular drive screens the front of the residence from the street. Landscape architect: Chandler D. Fairbank, Portland.*

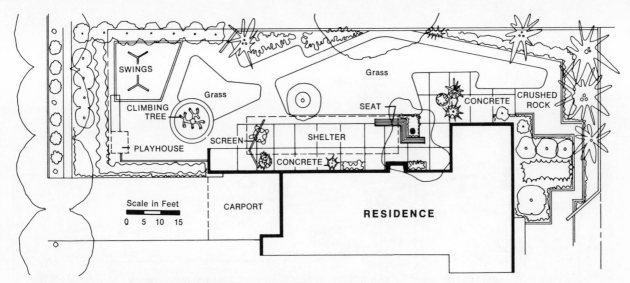

**GOOD LANDSCAPING "ENLARGES" A NARROW LOT** ● *Space needed for outdoor living as well as an outdoor play area for the children. The patio is covered, and is screened from the play area. Curving lines of the grass area and careful use of plant materials give the illusion of width. Landscape architect: Mary Gordon, Palo Alto, California.*

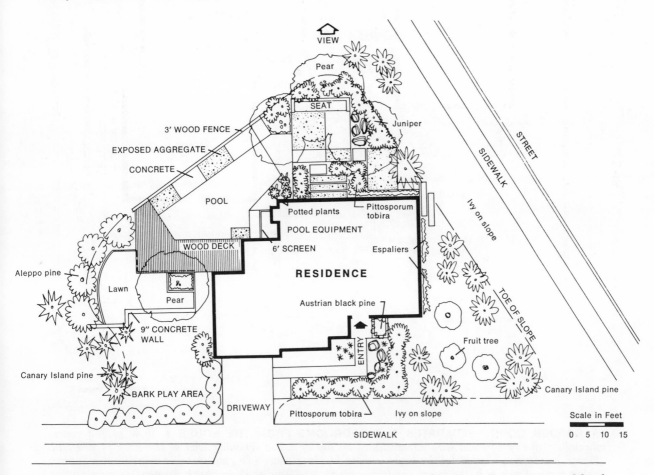

**CORNER LOT WITH A VIEW TO THE REAR** ● *This corner lot on a slope needed privacy, and level space for outdoor living and entertaining. The major view is to the rear of the property and is utilized by the creation of a patio area and built-in seat. Plants surround this area. The play area is placed in the front of the lot away from the pool. Landscape architect: Jon Myhre, Los Angeles.*

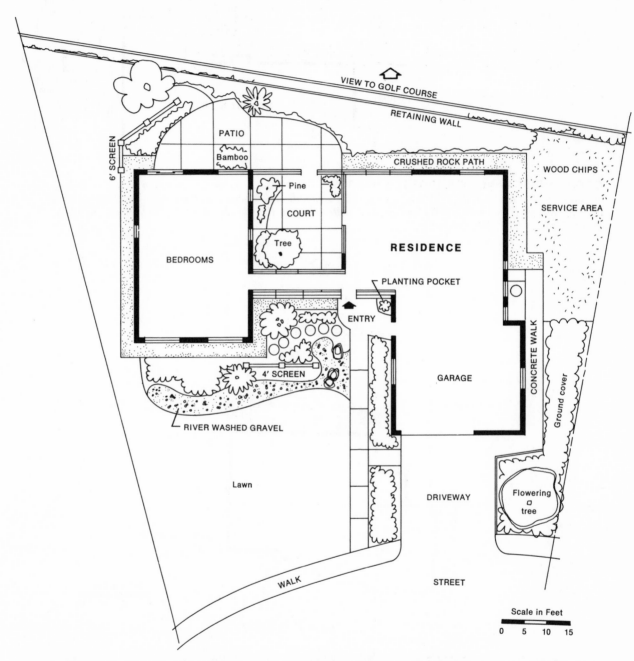

VIEW TO GOLF COURSE

RETAINING WALL

6' SCREEN

PATIO

Bamboo

CRUSHED ROCK PATH

WOOD CHIPS

SERVICE AREA

Pine

COURT

BEDROOMS

Tree

RESIDENCE

PLANTING POCKET

ENTRY

GARAGE

CONCRETE WALK

Ground cover

4' SCREEN

RIVER WASHED GRAVEL

Lawn

DRIVEWAY

Flowering tree

WALK

STREET

Scale in Feet

0   5   10   15

**A GARDEN COURT SEPARATES THE BEDROOMS FROM THE HOUSE** • *View of golf course through high wood-framed wire screen placed on top of a low retaining wall at the back of property. Partial privacy is provided by the fence without blocking view. The patio, interior court furnish outdoor living space. Lawn is in the front. Landscape architect: Chandler D. Fairbank, Portland.*

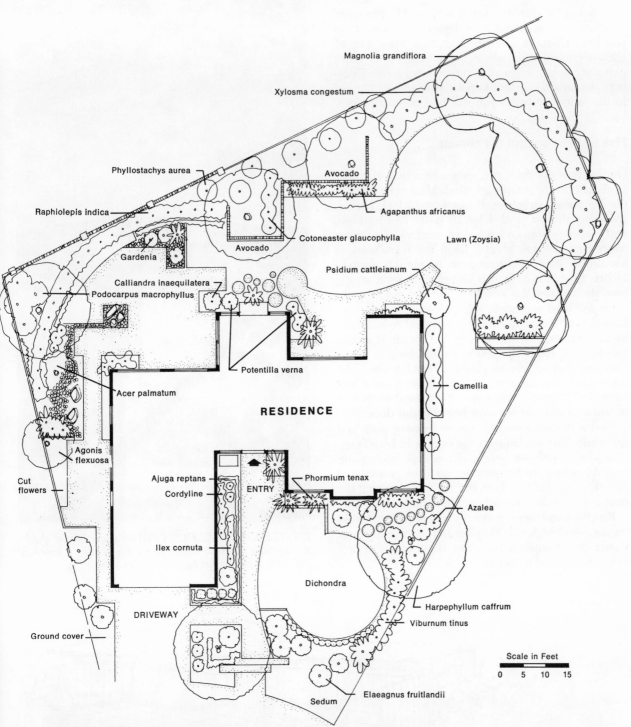

Magnolia grandiflora

Xylosma congestum

Phyllostachys aurea

Raphiolepis indica

Avocado

Agapanthus africanus

Cotoneaster glaucophylla

Gardenia

Avocado

Lawn (Zoysia)

Calliandra inaequilatera
Podocarpus macrophyllus

Psidium cattleianum

Potentilla verna

Acer palmatum

Camellia

RESIDENCE

Agonis
flexuosa

Ajuga reptans

Phormium tenax

Cut
flowers

Cordyline

ENTRY

Azalea

Ilex cornuta

Dichondra

Harpephyllum caffrum

DRIVEWAY

Viburnum tinus

Ground cover

Scale in Feet

0   5   10   15

Sedum

Elaeagnus fruitlandii

**LAWNS, CONCRETE AREAS, PLANTING BEDS FOR A CUL-DE-SAC LOT** • *Circles constitute the major theme for the landscaping of this cul-de-sac lot. This design carries the eye around the large back area of the property. A patio occupies one side of the lot while lawn, planting the remainder. Interesting use of rocks. Landscape architects: Jones/Peterson, Anaheim, California.*

## CLIMATE CONTROL

Your needs for climate control may vary from season to season, or may be different depending upon where you live. Chances are, however, that some sort of climate control will make living outdoors or in more pleasant. Below is an illustration, exaggerated perhaps, of how to control various elements of nature. In the following pages you will find other solutions.

### Five ways to control the climate

On this balcony deck you see an area in which five kinds of climate control are used. Most prominent is the big screen structure. It has 4 by 12-inch beams, spanning 19 feet, and 4 by 10 posts 19 feet high, with splice plates and other connectors of maintenance-free stainless steel. Lining the framework is aluminum insect screening in aluminum frames. Debris that falls on it can be removed by a strong hose stream from the balcony.

On the west and north sides, removable panels of heavy sheet vinyl control the breeze and reduce sunlight. To prevent wind-ripping, the plastic is bound around the edges in heavy canvas, which holds fasteners that attach the panels to the framing. The framework also supports a roof extension out 6 feet from the existing house eaves, for a total of 9½ feet of sun and rain shelter over balcony and deck.

Under the screening, a canvas awning pulls out for shade. The section over the deck is 12 by 20 feet. The wire suspension system allows neat folding and easy retracting. In the picture, note the grommeted rain drainage holes at bottom fold lines; keeping the canvas dry under the roof overhang prolongs its life.

Finally, two louvered storm shutters slide in tracks on the 3-foot-high sill. They break the force of storm winds, predominantly from the south, and also provide privacy and a measure of shade.

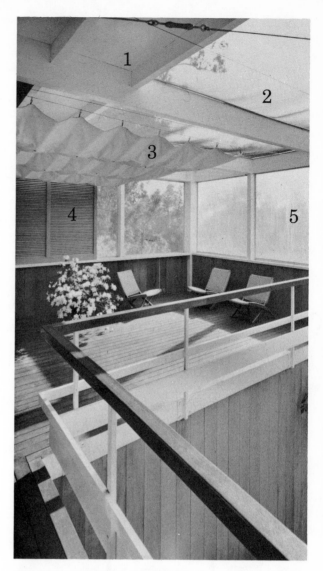

*ENVIRONMENTAL CONTROL: 1 overhang for shade, 2 screening for insects, 3 canvas for shade, 4 louvered shutters, 5 plastic for breeze control.*

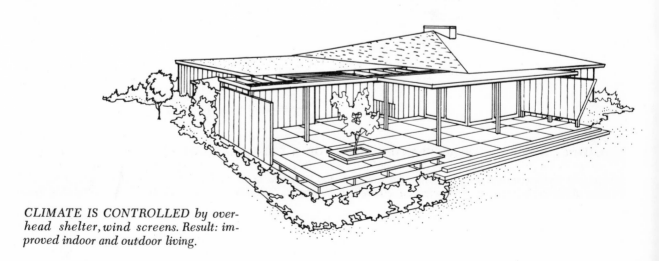

*CLIMATE IS CONTROLLED by overhead shelter, wind screens. Result: improved indoor and outdoor living.*

## Garden houses to check the wind

The two garden houses shown on this page were built to provide some sort of climate control to make them habitable. Both have overhead lath to give welcome shade for people and plants. The wind is checked by glass in one case and by white plastic panels in the other. The structure at the right has removable windows so that the house can be made more open if desired. Air circulation is provided for in both of these rooms so that the cooling breezes may pass through.

*WIND'S COMING UP, plastic windows put in. Frames secured by turn buttons. Ten windows removable.*

*AMPLE AIR CIRCULATION is provided for, even with windows in place. Design: William Kapranos.*

*VIEW IS ENJOYED without the wind. The structure is large enough so even the unsheltered parts of the garden benefit. Without it the garden would be rather windswept. Design: N. Bob Murakami.*

*STRONG WIND is checked by panels of glass and hardboard. Shade plants thrive on outside of the garden house.*

## Doors to modify the climate

Eight doors modify the climate in this interior court, protecting the plants and outdoor sitting area from prevailing winds, folding back to open the court to the mountain view. This house is located so that the winds out of the Sierra blow into the court, winds which can be strong and chilly. The doors can be used to equally good advantage at the beach, though you may want to use more glass in the doors so you don't obscure the ocean view; at a vacation house as a security factor; or even on a small suburban lot to increase privacy as well as modify the climate.

Below, pivoting patio screens for sun control.

DOORS OPEN so that the distant mountains become a part of the court garden. Design: Germano Milono.

DOORS CLOSE to stop the wind that often blows out of the mountains. The eight doors lock on the inside.

PIVOTING FIBERGLASS SCREENS are inexpensive to build, and can be turned and adjusted easily. Here, they are fully open. Designer: Gregory Mull.

PIVOTS are made of galvanized 20-penny nails with the ends cut off. The upper screw eye holds the pin when it is not needed. Screens are very lightweight.

## Louvers for shade—to block the wind

Here are two examples of louvers which can be opened or closed as indicated by the weather. Opening the louvers will allow the breeze to blow through when desired, or will filter sunlight in interesting patterns. Not only do these panels serve as functional climate controls, but as the photograph at the right illustrates, the appearance of the house is vastly improved.

The louvers fit in a framework of 2 by 6's, and the slats are 1 by 6 panels that pivot on 6 by ¼-inch stove bolts, with washers at top and bottom. The control rod keeps them parallel.

*TOP BAR (1 by 1 stock) keeps the louvers parallel. The bar also serves to open and to close them.*

*LOUVERED PANEL is 22 feet long by 7½ feet high. It shades wall, planter, and window. Design: G. C. Hayes.*

*OPEN, the hinged louvers let light in and cooling breezes through. Louvers move freely and are placed on the side of the fence from which unwanted winds blow.*

*CLOSED, the louvered fence cuts down the air flow of the unwanted east wind. Small brass hinges hold 1 by 6-inch slats to top and bottom. Design: Dan L. Rowland.*

## Intercept the sun outside the glass

The best place to stop or diffuse the rays of the sun is outside the house wall. Shown on this page are several good ways to intercept the sun outdoors with screens of wood and canvas.

Wood is excellent, provided that it is compatible with the architecture of your home. It requires little care and no daily adjustment. Canvas is more versatile—it can be stretched on a frame, rolled down, folded out—and you can get gaily-colored canvas that will withstand the weather for many years without fading.

*ROOF EXTENSION shades the windows below. The louvers are 4 feet wide. Design: Dan L. Rowland.*

*VERTICAL WOOD SCREEN also shades. This one is made of 5-foot-long 2 by 2's. Design: Paul Sterling Hoag.*

*CANVAS can be left up for the view, rolled down whenever shade is desired in rooms. Design: Richard J. Neutra.*

*ON WIDE ROOF OVERHANG, canvas shades. They needn't reach the floor. Design: Hendrick and Mock.*

## A fabric sun shade

Here's a sun control that uses wide bands of a canvaslike material in a rather whimsical, sawtooth manner. Spanning one end of a deck, it is designed so its four vertical supports also hold up the deck. Its slim silhouette doesn't interfere with the view. Woven over and under two levels of pipe, the material is kept taut so it doesn't flap in the wind or sag over its 16-foot span. A 21-inch-wide bench is built into the deck railing around the three sides.

After three years, the original canvas was replaced by a synthetic material made of fade-resistant acrylic fiber. The strips are removed each winter. All you do is unlash the ropes that hold the three strips to the pipe on each end, then fold and store the material.

*DECK JOINS LOWER GARDEN by a flight of steps. House right. Design: Royston, Hanamoto, Mayes & Beck.*

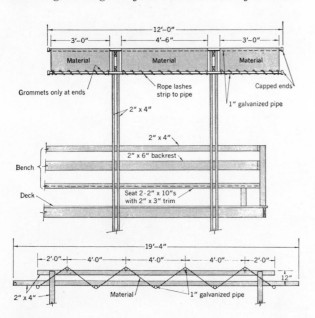

*FINISHED LOOK is given by caps on pipe ends. They also serve to keep the canvas from slipping off.*

*DECK BECOMES SHADED TREE HOUSE by day. At night it is lighted by four hanging cylindrical lights.*

# Gardens for Dedicated Gardeners

Gardeners who are interested in special plants are concerned with acquiring more space for their special interest. Though overall design may not be their primary concern, the most effective way to handle favorites is to design a garden that looks good without them. By designing a basic framework that is attractive throughout the year, you automatically provide the most attractive background.

Most of the gardens presented in this book would be suitable. However, we have selected a few gardens belonging to people who love plants and specialize in particular favorites to give you additional ideas.

Keep in mind that as garden living increases its demand for space, and paving or hard surfaces take over larger areas, the opportunities for exciting, more concentrated use of plant material increase. When dining, loafing, and reading move out into the garden, the relationship between plants and people becomes more intimate. With raised beds, seat walls, tubs, boxes, and planters, you find yourself closer to your plants than in a walk through a garden. This, too, offers the gardener new challenges.

## A GARDEN FOR ONE WHO LIKES PLANTS

The garden pictured here was planned and executed by the owner. The basic design of the garden has strong structural shapes that are continually being softened by the growth of the plant material. Essentially, this is a garden for someone who likes plants.

*BRICK PATH along side of the house narrows to accommodate curving raised bed around large oak. Fatsia, left. More about this garden on pages 36-37.*

The garden occupies a half-acre; sheltered from the wind and hot sun, only a few miles from the ocean with its occasional fogs and high overcast, it has some of the climatic and environmental aspects and much of the feeling of the cool tropics. Native live oak trees and sycamores form a high leafy canopy that throws a beautiful pattern of sun and shade. Background plantings in mass, with only occasional accents, are in keeping with the natural surroundings. In close-up situations one finds more variation and detail.

Although plants in shades of green predominate in this woodland garden, there are subtle contrasts with such gray foliaged plants as silvery, fine-textured Australian cushion bush (*Calocephalus brownii*), tropical-looking rice paper plant (*Tetrapanax papyriferus*), and succulents.

All the rocks used in the garden were found on the site, mainly along the stream. They range in size from pebbles to massive boulders, many beautifully patterned with lichen. Bracken fern, which grows wild in the canyon, has been allowed to become part of the scheme in many parts of the garden. Stepping stones and material used in some of the low retaining walls are pieces of rubble that were left when the city installed curbstones along the roadways in the old downtown area.

The house is very nearly surrounded by terraces and paths paved with bricks laid in sand. One of their important functions is to provide an even surface for tricycling by two small girls.

The basically green and gray garden derives seasonal color accents from permanent plants such as agapanthus, bergenia, and ajuga. In the greenhouse and lathhouse, the owners grow many of their own plants from seeds and cuttings, and bring on many plants—azaleas, hydrangeas, tuberous begonias, and others—in containers. One of their current projects is growing staghorn ferns from spores.

*DRIFTWOOD GRAY HOUSE is enclosed by garden which fits quietly into the wooded canyon setting. Good environment for tropical plants. Asphalt parking area. Native rocks on site. Designer: John W. Pitman.*

*BORDER SEEN on left contains Australian tree ferns, bergenia, Hahn's ivy. Hanging globe lights area.*

*STUDY IN FORM, texture, color: rosettes of Agave attenuata, fern, donkey tail sedum, ajuga, bark.*

*SUNNY OPEN TERRACE provides space for family outdoor living. Bold, lustrous-leafed acanthus against the house. Ajuga ground cover. Above retaining wall are agapanthus, bergenia, ferns, ivy.*

*NATIVE BRACKEN FERN, abundant in canyon, allowed to remain in this retreat at the edge of woodland; pulled up where out of bounds. Ajuga, helxine is between the stones; zoysia at right.*

*SMALL-SCALE GARDEN provides green world at every season. It is enjoyable from the protected patio as well as the living room and kitchen. The collection of plants and shrubs is well displayed.*

## GARDEN PLANTED ON MOUNDS

This garden is planted on a series of earth mounds formed from good garden soil. Because of poor drainage, gardening here was impossible and the mounds of earth became the solution. The owners spread gravel on the clay between the mounds to make the paths which lead to all parts of the garden. The mounds make a handsome setting for the collection of shrubs and trees. This garden is particularly attractive when lighted at night both in winter and summer.

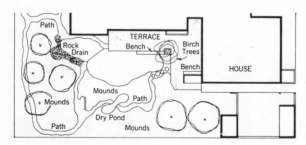

*PLAN shows paths between planting beds; they meander through back yard and provide for water runoff.*

*RAISED CEDAR ROUNDS provide stepping places to keep your feet dry after heavy rains. Attractive texture.*

## GARDENING ON A DECK

One of the drawbacks of gardening on a deck is that you're usually restricted to growing plants in tubs or pots. Here we show a way to do it on a greater scale.

The garden consists of six 4 by 6-foot planter boxes set along one side of a waterside deck (see sketch). They are filled with topsoil and planted with a selection of succulents and conifers. Since this represents a good deal of extra weight, the deck should be designed accordingly. But you can lessen the load somewhat by using a planting mix of sand and peat moss or a U. C. mix (a lightweight, porous soil mix made up of fine sand or perlite combined with peat moss, sawdust, or ground bark to which fertilizer has been added).

Holes in the bottom of each planter box allow excess water to drain down under the deck.

*SUCCULENTS make the major planting in the boxes; they are attractive to look down upon.*

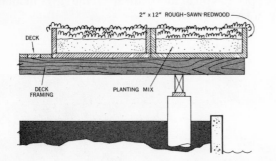

*PLANTING BOXES of this size, used in a double row, eliminate the need for a safety railing along middle portion of the deck. Their low height does not obstruct the view. Design: Michael Siegel and Helen Selby.*

## AN ALMOST ALL-EUCALYPTUS GARDEN

These photographs show a garden in which the owners placed and matched eucalypts throughout their garden. Such a job could have had rather gloomy results because there are many kinds of eucalyptus and unless you know the potentials of the various rare kinds you could accidentally put together some incongruous companions. But these people studied their Blakely (*A Key to the Eucalypts*, by W. F. Blakely) and companion volumes well, and subsequently did a splendid job of placing and matching kinds.

The photographs shown on this page show only the species that the owners placed in the highly-used parts of their garden—patio and entry. On the slopes beyond the house stand many strapping young saplings of the more familiar big-eucalypt class. Along the entrance drive they used many plants of a popular species sold at most nurseries: the silver mountain gum (*E. pulverulenta*).

*VIEW FROM BACK of patio. Circle contains* Eucalyptus preissiana, *and* E. spathulata. *In back* E. miniata.

*ENTRY to eucalyptus collectors' home. By front door,* E. erythrocorys; *trained on wall,* E. rhodantha.

*REAR PATIO is enclosed on three sides by house, on fourth by covered pool. Left of bench,* E. preissiana.

*UPPER TERRACE. Orange tree in round bed, rear, was one of two existing trees when owners began planting. Heavy roofing paper under rock keeps weeds out. Ice plant bank cover also discourages weeds.*

## AN UNUSUAL GARDEN

This garden breaks several cardinal rules in the contemporary landscaping rule-book. Yet for all its uninhibited qualities, it is a pleasure to walk through and to look at. Furthermore, it offers some useful landscaping lessons.

The chief rule that was broken is the one that says trees should be spaced according to their ultimate size. That interesting little waist-high forest of palm trees in the photograph on this page will become a crowded jungle of interwoven fronds in several years. But the owners will solve that problem somehow when the time comes, if the problem doesn't solve itself in the meantime. For one thing, they say, when the dichondra lawn gets shaded out by the overlapping palm tops, they may start raising orchids and ferns beneath them.

*PALM FOREST contains 326 trees. Owners love trees, especially palms, will let tomorrow take care of itself.*

## SHADE FOR SHADE PLANTS

Getting shade plants to grow or bloom well in summer in hot dry areas is likely to be a struggle. But you can modify this climate by screening the plants from wind, giving them filtered shade, and supplying the needed air moisture or humidity with misting devices or sprinklers. On this page are several illustrations.

*STEEL OVERHEAD structure for the garden holds sliding panels of shade cloth easily arranged for shade.*

*PLANTS AND PEOPLE benefit from this shelter. It's 54 feet long, 10 feet deep, 7½ feet high in front.*

*LATHHOUSE PLANT DISPLAY area provided by egg-crate overhead. Storage closet, bins contain supplies.*

*FAR END of shelter shown above. Watering of pots, hanging baskets, and hosing of pavement raise humidity.*

*RAISED BED or retaining wall of rocks is an effective way of displaying plants. Spaces between the rocks provide pockets in which additional plants may be grown. Natural feeling is retained.*

## NEAT GARDEN ISLANDS

Put a tree in a raised bed, underplant it with annuals, perennials, or low growing shrubs, and you create a combination that may well be the focal point of the entire garden. Here in the photographs are two examples.

The tree-and-raised-bed combination also gives you an area to dress up. It is an ideal spot for choice miniatures that require the shade of a tree, giving them more importance by bringing them closer to eye level. It forms a display area for a concentration of color throughout the year—azaleas and spring bulbs, summer annuals, showy chrysanthemums—or for a piece of garden sculpture. Raised beds are not only decorative, but also practical. Plants are protected from damage; the walls retain water, functioning as a watering basin.

Coarse bark can be spread on the bare ground to give a neat appearance to the plantings and prevent mud from being splashed on plants.

*PUT A TREE in raised bed, and underplant it with annuals, perennials, or low shrubs. Design: Richard Beeson.*

# Gardens for Casual Gardeners

Casual gardeners come in many grades. There's the person who has never gardened, is afraid of gardening, and doesn't want to study gardening or plants. "All I want," he says, "is to get a pleasant outdoor room. I suppose there will have to be some plants, but they should be the kind that can almost take care of themselves."

A more complex type of casual gardener is represented by the young couple trying to keep in balance a growing interest in gardening. They find themselves delighted with gardening, but having to give more and more time to it and less to reading, weekend trips, visiting with friends. They want a garden "that demands no more than its rightful portion of our free time."

Another type is the overly ambitious gardener who started from scratch three years ago and has done such a wonderful job that neighbors and friends shower him with praise. He has given his project every spare moment of every day in the last three years. Suddenly he feels that the garden has trapped him. He is sick and tired of it. He is sure that to keep it in its present state of perfection will allow for no letdown—ever.

While all casual gardeners have in common a desire to cut down garden work, they don't mean it when the say they are willing to give up all garden interest. After demanding a landscape plan without space for growing things, they may in a very short time develop a keen interest in every phase of gardening and may find themselves wondering why they ever insisted upon anything as dull as a minimum-maintenance garden plan.

Of course, there is no such thing as a work-free

SLOPE PLANTING. Lemonade berry, top right, with Carmel creeper directly below, Acacia longifolia, center, on left of path. More about garden—page 49.

garden. As long as there are plants of any kind, there will be work to do.

Over the years we have often been asked to prepare a check list on the relative amount of time required for certain typical garden tasks so that the home owner could look down the list and avoid, or select, features that will absorb his time. There are real traps in such lists. "Relative amount of time" is deceiving. You may have to water a flower pot every day and weed a flower bed every month. If you are next to the flower pot every day and water is within reach, you will spend less time on it than you do on the monthly weeding. To place only a time value on weeding is not very realistic, either. If oxalis starts to overrun the garden, or quack grass or Bermuda grass has a foothold, weeding not only takes time but frays tempers.

As a class, vegetables take semi-weekly attention while they are young, and dusting when attacked by insects or disease. But swiss chard, zucchini, and corn are not at all demanding of time.

A gravel path must be weeded and raked frequently if you insist on spic-and-span neatness. But with some tolerance and an occasional spraying with diesel oil, the gravel path drops out of the high maintenance class. Time and effort in garden work depends more on the efficiency of layout and equipment than on anything else.

Roses, supposedly, are in the high-maintenance class because of spraying, pruning, watering, and weeding. But doesn't it depend on the rose? We have seen large border plantings of floribundas that required little care other than winter pruning.

Here is a list of the tasks that must be performed in a small garden.

1. Hedge: Must be clipped often to be kept neat.
2. Annual border: Changed two or three times a year; weeded regularly; plants spill over lawn.
3. Espaliers: Need weekly attention during growing season.

4. Lawn: Walk divides into two narrow strips, multiplies edging and hand clipping tasks; design of walk encourages traffic to cut across corner.

5. Gravel from path gets into lawn, lawn mower.

6. Tree: Leaves falling on ground cover of sedum can't be raked, don't wash off easily.

7. Plant border and ground-cover area must be edged by spade.

Here is the same space redesigned for minimum maintenance:

1. Raised bed, planted with informal, free-growing shrubs requires little attention.

2. Mowing strip of brick or wood eliminates hand trimming of lawn.

3. New arrangement of lawn area cuts the edging job in half.

4. Tight-growing ground cover like ajuga or strawberry is easy to wash off with hose. Mounding juniper would allow the leaves to sift down out of sight—reducing cleanup.

5. Tree with small thin leaves is choice here. Leaves practically disappear.

6. Note that upkeep is reduced by changes in design more than in plant material.

Anyone interested in minimum maintenance should not overlook raised beds and mowing strips.

## RAISED BEDS

The raised bed gives a permanent clean line between the grass panel and the flowers and shrubs. It gives the gardener a free choice as to what he wants to do with annual color. If he elects to plant a spring border, he can enjoy that without worrying about bare ground in late summer, fall, and winter—the raised bed masks the bare dirt.

Built up beds are back savers. They are easier to weed, cultivate, and water. In gardens where there is a problem soil—too shallow or heavy, or poorly drained—the built-up bed filled with your special mix of top soil, sawdust, manure, or whatever, will change frustration and hard work into the pleasure of watching things grow. In areas where Bermuda grass is a problem, the built-up planting area almost does away with that terrible fight to keep Bermuda grass from taking over.

## MOWING STRIP

At the base of the built-up bed bordering the lawn, a 2 by 6 between the lawn and the raised bed acts as a mowing strip. Grass is kept away from the bed; only an occasional edging is necessary. Other uses of these devices are to be seen in photographs here and throughout the book.

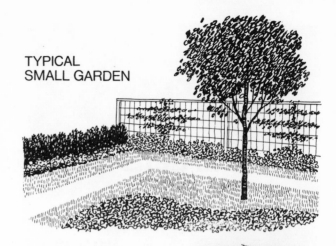

TYPICAL SMALL GARDEN

REDESIGNED FOR LOW MAINTENANCE

*MOWING STRIP of concrete continued around fence that juts out to separate garden. Design: Thomas Church.*

VEGETABLE BEDS, *raised. Wide paths edged with* *redwood. Design: Eckbo, Royston & Williams.*

BRICK EXTENDS *from porch for easy-to-sweep corner* *with raised bed. Design: Eric Armstrong, Jane Taylor.*

## CHILDREN AND MAINTENANCE

The same kind of planning as just described to reduce upkeep will result in more livable gardens for children. The raised bed prevents damage from wheels, bikes, and dogs. No dirt washes into paths if the facing plank is properly installed. The unifying of lawn and paving areas gives more play space. There is no pick-up of gravel on shoes. However, if you believe that children have a right to play in the soil, don't pave all of the play yard.

### What is work and what is play?

Gardeners interested in minimum maintenance should remember this psychological quirk in garden work: A job that you can complete in half an hour seems easier than a half hour's work in a border that takes hours to make shipshape. This happens where the garden is marked off in several small areas rather than long borders. Dressing up only one area gives the garden an immediate lift and gives the gardener a big reward for a little attention.

When looking for ways to cut down work in the garden, don't rush into planting changes, hoping that there are plants that will take care of themselves. When a magazine, a book, or a friend talks about low maintenance material, they are talking about a relative thing. For example, ground covers as lawn substitutes will change your work from cutting to weeding. But hours per month may be the same or more. Weeds enjoy growing in strawberry; grass seeds itself in thyme and Irish moss. About the only exceptions to the weedy rule are ivy and juniper, and they take time to reach the point where they completely cover the ground.

Enlarging paved areas and cutting down slightly on lawn areas saves practically no labor. Once the lawn mower is under way, the difference between cutting 3,000 square feet and 3,500 square feet is negligible. It does make a lot of difference how the lawn areas are arranged. Small patches, half circles, or strips of lawn are annoying to cut and edge.

Don't pin your hopes for low upkeep on perennials. You may not have to plant them each year, but they do have to be cut back, or divided, or confined. Not even shrubs can be counted on to behave as they should without attention. If they are to remain attractive over the years they must be pruned, or thinned, or shaped, fed, watered, raked up beneath, staked, and sometimes sprayed.

It has been suggested that the way to plan a low maintenance garden is to start on paper with a completely paved garden and remove sections here and there for the plantings you regard as minimum for beauty and comfort. Perhaps a better way would be to regard a few hours' upkeep each week as play.

Here and on the following pages are some ideas for gardens requiring minimum maintenance.

![Fruitless mulberry shades pool by family room]

FRUITLESS MULBERRY *shades pool by family room. Purple-leafed ajuga at base, combined with bamboo.*

## THIS GARDEN ALMOST TAKES CARE OF ITSELF

To keep a garden looking crisp and fresh through long, hot summers in a hot climate requires well adapted plants, and in addition you must normally provide a great deal of special care. But the owners of the house pictured here wanted a garden that would require little maintenance. So heat-tolerant plants that are easy to grow were used. Interesting foliage combinations were also heavily relied upon.

Flowers in orange shades provide the principal color accents; these include bird-of-paradise, clivia, dwarf flowering pomegranate, 'Copper King' gazania, 'Mojave' rose, and scarlet wisteria trees, which are planted along the top of the mound.

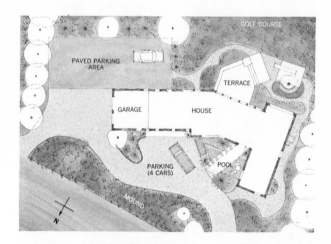

![Privacy from road provided by prostrate junipers]

PRIVACY FROM ROAD *provided by prostrate junipers. Umbrella plant by stairs. Design: Leo Schuster.*

ROUNDED TUFTS *of blue fescue cover ground. Nandina, center; juniper, right; Yucca filamentosa, left.*

*ENTRYWAY flanked by two trailing rosemary plants. Tall trees provide shade and interest. Garden has a feeling of rustic informality. Natives heavily relied upon. Design: Thomas C. Moore.*

## LITTLE WATER AND LITTLE WORK

To give this hillside garden a feeling of rustic informality, provide privacy, and make it as easy to maintain as possible, native plants were heavily relied upon; combined with them were other kinds requiring very little special care once established. All the shrubs that were used in mass planting—namely the Carmel creeper (*Ceanothus griseus horizontalis*), lemonade berry (*Rhus integrifolia*), sugar bush (*R. ovata*), and the bushy form of acacia (*A. longifolia*, often sold as *A. latifolia*)—were planted from gallon cans and spaced 8 feet apart. These four plants are broad-leafed evergreens.

After the basic planting was completed, a mixture of California wildflower seeds was sown to cover the bare ground between and help hold the soil. Within three years the shrubs had grown together and formed a complete covering.

The garden has required little care, aside from regular but infrequent watering (about once a month) and just enough pruning to keep plant growth clear of the paths.

*VIEW DOWN PATH that leads to terrace (shown on page 44). Lemonade berry screens area from road.*

*FRONT ENTRANCE reached by wide steps from parking area. Slope planted with heather, and lower growing, succulent-leafed sedums. Many rhododendrons and azaleas in garden. Design: Glen Hunt.*

*WOODEN PLATFORM around madrone tree doubles as bench and table. Also serves as base for sleeping bags.*

## ON AN ACRE . . .

Around their roomy, comfortable house on an acre-sized lot the owners of this house hoped for a garden that would enhance the natural beauty of the madrone grove that dominates their house and lot. They also wanted a minimum of upkeep, and a garden that could withstand the active play of three youngsters and their friends.

With these requirements in mind, a design was developed to provide easy-to-maintain surfaces close to the house: wood decking, gravel, and paving. Many kinds of shrubs, mostly broad-leafed evergreens, make the garden interesting at every season. Rhododendrons under tall madrones serve as transition plants between the garden sections and the woods with their natural undergrowth of salal and bracken ferns.

In a neighborhood where paved sidewalks may not be installed for years, a 3-foot wide asphalt path for bicycling and roller skating now curves through the woods, roughly following the perimeter of the lot. A paved area around the fire-pit is a favorite meeting place for a group of 10-year-old Campfire Girls. A screen supplies privacy here and keeps off the wind. The Boy Scout and Cub Scout of the family choose to hold meetings in a tree house, or in secret camps set up in the woods.

LOW STONE wall behind fire-pit on patio serves as raised bench. Protection provided by the wood screens.

LOOKING from the house toward back of property, you see shadowy grove of madrones. It is a woodland retreat.

VIEW OF REAR GARDEN. This area planned for use of a large family. Large paved section has been the scene of dances, theatricals. Overhead trellis extends over deck which serves for outdoor dining.

GOLDEN BAMBOO *fills the corner at the bottom of the stairs leading to deck. Deck off the second-floor master bedroom and sitting room overlooks the garden. Lanai and dining room are under the deck.*

PATH LEADS *to wisteria-covered arbor, then through gate to swimming pool area in rear of the garden.*

## A NEW SIMPLE GARDEN REPLACES AN OLD ONE

This garden replaced a very different original garden established 50 years earlier. The original consisted of a conglomeration of paths, oddly shaped flower and shrub beds, and a large rectangular lawn.

The new garden was planned along simple lines, and planted almost exclusively with shrubs in differing shades of green, with varying textures and leaf patterns. Pots of coral geraniums, and coral-colored cushions that pick up the warm tones of the brick in the benches and wall provide the main warm color accents.

The 1,400-square-foot terrace, laid out in 4 by 6-foot rectangles of exposed aggregate concrete, loops around the large oak tree and in front of the lanai and dining room. The benches were built of bricks from the old paths.

The arbor at the rear of the garden was extended at each end to bring it into scale with the enlarged garden. Behind the arbor is a large California pepper tree (*Schinus molle*), an especially handsome focal point when night-lighted to dramatize its high, gnarled branches.

*PANELS of gray santolina, green Japanese boxwood border the path. White marguerites behind. Azara is trained against the fence. Exposed aggregate concrete walk connects with the patio.*

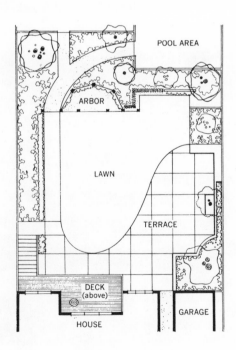

*PLAN VIEW shows the simple lines and the spacious character of the remodeled garden.*

*SIMPLE LINES of garden stand out clearly from vantage point on deck. Exposed aggregate terrace.*

## NATIVES . . . FOR AN ALMOST CAREFREE GARDEN

Native trees, shrubs, ground covers, and ferns can do some wonderful and surprising things to make a new home blend with its surroundings. They soften the raw, unfinished look while relating the house both to distant views and to adjoining properties. And if the planting is done with care and nursed along for the first couple of years, the result is a virtually carefree garden.

Native plants are accustomed to getting along with conditions as they are. They don't need fertilizers (in fact, commercial fertilizers will damage or kill many natives) or copious summer watering, once they catch on and begin to grow. However, they will eventually need thinning and cutting back to keep them within bounds.

*TROUGH of gravel and rocks provides drainage at dripline. Sword ferns thrive against north wall.*

*GRAVEL PATH curves from street to front entrance. Banks of evergreen kinnikinnick and greasewood.*

*EARTH MOUNDS planted with native shrubs and ground covers give depth and privacy to front yard.*

*STEPS of railroad ties lead to front door from parking area. Design: Esther Pearson and Clayton James.*

## YEAR-AROUND GOOD LOOKS

Sometimes you can build a garden around a framework of only half a dozen kinds of plants and have it as good looking in January as in July. The photographs and the plan on this page illustrate such an example.

Big sweeps of 14 xylosmas, 19 star jasmines, and 12 nandinas might be expected to seem monotonous in an area only 64 by 50 feet; but they actually do a better job of holding the garden design together than if many more kinds of plants were used. And many shades of foliage are represented, from lettuce-greens to blackish greens.

The garden was five years old when these photographs were taken. Now that plants are well established, maintenance is pretty much a matter of grooming and watering.

*PURPLELEAF PLUMS grow between xylosma and fence in area kept weed free but unplanted.*

*RAISED BED of star jasmine lines the patio. Fence serves as screen for privacy, division of garden space.*

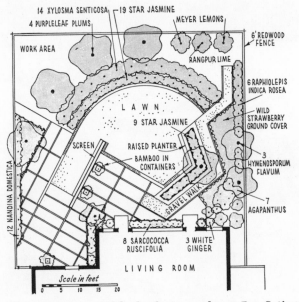

*PLAN was prepared by landscape architect Roy Seifert. This section of the garden is 64 by 50 feet.*

*LOOKING DOWN from the roof, you can see the entire yard. Note informal planting of xylosma near lawn.*

# Landscaping Your Site for Beauty and Function

Your site falls by virtue of function into several distinct though related areas—streetside gardens, play areas, living areas. The requirements of your family may place importance on one over the others; for example, the garden of a family with small children may tend toward more play space than living space. While function cannot be denied, the need for pleasant sensory experiences should be considered.

We have collected many ideas for each area in this chapter. Keep in mind your family's changing needs as you plan or seek new ideas. Small children grow up quickly; tricycles change to bicycles, sandboxes to basketball hoops. You may also change your feelings about the amount of space that you want to devote to raising plants. If changing needs are kept in mind as you plan, drastic remodeling may be saved later. Ideas for family games and activities, and adult games are also presented.

## STREETSIDE GARDENS

Planning or remodeling the front "public" garden generally calls for a set of considerations different from landscaping the private back yard. The streetside garden is on view for all who pass by, and is in constant view of your neighbors. But you don't want to get trapped into spending all your garden time and money in an area you can't use. Low maintenance is an important factor in streetside planting consideration.

Perhaps you would like to set your house apart from the others in the block. In a new subdivision where houses are all the same age and much alike in appearance, the desire for individuality is a natural one. If the public area is extensive because of an unusually deep setback, as in many older neighborhoods, you may want to take back some of the public space and work out a front patio.

First, let's look at the problem in a subdivision where houses have identical setbacks and a series of driveways at exact right angles to the street. In such a situation, if you wish to set yourself apart from the neighbors, you must think of two problems simultaneously. Your plan must work as a unit with the house and at the same time break up the uniform pattern of the street. Let's look at both aspects of this problem.

The quickest way to break the uniformity of a subdivision street is to work with strong vertical elements such as hedges or rows of trees. Fences, high for privacy or low for the division of space, and raised plant beds, will quickly vary the over-all appearance of the street.

The change from lawn to ground cover breaks the uniform pattern, especially if the ground covers are selected to create interest by contrasting textures and colors. Planting with ground covers, confining plants with header boards to prevent intermingling, offers the bold gardener many opportunities for individual expression. Couple plantings with wide paths and generous paving, and the departure from other homes on the street is even more pronounced.

The parking strip takes well to imaginative ground cover treatment. This area offers visitors a preliminary welcome. Make some provision for foot traffic—a dry, paved area adjacent to the parking area.

You may want to change the stiff line established by your driveway. This can be done in several ways. Put a raised bed on one side of the driveway with low planting on the other side, or pave a step-out strip along the driveway and then join this strip to the entry walk with a generous area of paving.

*SCREENS for privacy partly enclose garden court and present interesting patterns from streetside. The combination of the screens changes the looks of the house.*

## Coordinate front landscaping with neighbors

When neighbors act together, it is possible to achieve a high degree of landscape harmony—particularly of front gardens. The photographs shown on these two pages illustrate such a coordination while still reflecting the individual tastes of owners.

One family had small children and needed an enclosed yard; the other preferred less privacy and chose see-through grillework. Although three fence designs are used, the fences are coordinated by the same material and color. Outside the fences, a ground cover planting runs along the front of both lots to provide continuity.

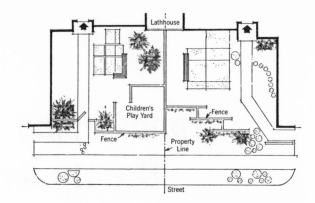

*NEIGHBORING front gardens are identical in size, separated by property-line fence. Lathhouse, between.*

*CONTINUOUS FENCE on one property encloses front garden where children play; louvered around entry, solid to hide play yard. Wooden rounds serve as dry stepping places. Design: Frederick M. Lang.*

OPENWORK SCREENS *flank entrance to the neighboring house. In combination with planting, they create privacy without blocking view. Stepping stones here are of concrete and tie in with rounds next door.*

SHADOWBOX FENCE *made from 1 by 10's and 1 by 4's is attractive from both sides.*

ADJOINING FENCE *employs a series of rough-finished redwood 1 by 4's fastened to short 2 by 4 spacers.*

*BEFORE remodel, house lacked privacy. Narrow drive, and restricted view made backing car dangerous.*

## Make the front garden an entrance court

Whether you want to set your house apart from the neighbors' or to cut down on public garden maintenance, one of the best approaches is to consider the front garden as an entrance court—either in part or using the entire area. The conventional approach that concentrates on the front of the house as an architectural unit to be enhanced by shrub and tree planting fails to work when houses are so closely joined that it is impossible to look at them as individual units.

By concentrating on an entrance court and forgetting the face of the house for the moment, you are likely to end up with an attractive entry garden that takes care of all the foundation planting generally associated with landscaping the front of the house. Your planning should start with the correction of any awkward situation caused by the house itself. These are the kinds of problems you may face:

How to get out of a car without stepping on grass or planting?

What to do when a front picture window or a wall of glass looks out on your entry garden?

How to help guests reach the entrance easily from both the street and driveway?

What to do with the narrow walk from sidewalk to front door?

In the photographs that follow there are several different approaches to using the front garden as an entry court.

The house pictured here was remodeled to accomplish two purposes: To provide off-street parking and to screen off a private area on the sunny front of the house. Two thirds of the front lawn were surfaced to park as many as four cars. Three tall baffles, each 12 feet wide, screen the house from the street. Behind the baffles, a generous paved patio easily accommodates lawn chairs and a picnic table. A planting bay breaks the expanse of paving and there is a 4-foot-wide shrub bed between the house and the patio.

*AFTER. Three tall baffles, each 12 feet wide, screen house from parking area. Behind them, paved patio.*

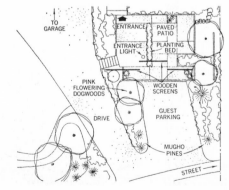

*PLAN SHOWS new parking area near street and a patio in front of the house. Design: Glen Hunt.*

## Another entrance court

Here is a good example of a combined house and streetside remodel. Because of the deep setback, it was possible to extend the house to the front, and a new entry court was included in the remodeling.

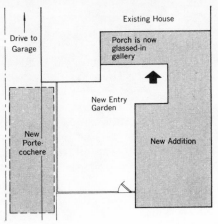

PLAN. *New bedroom wing separate from other bedroom area has view of garden. Design: John Gerard.*

BEFORE. *The house was originally 36 feet away from the street, with drive on the left side.*

ENTRY GARDEN *made from porch. View from living room, adjoining new entry, looks toward front.*

AFTER. *Addition is about 14½ feet from street. Porte-cochère over driveway, entry, new bedroom.*

*AFTER. Raised bed and shrubbery now separate the driveway from the front entrance wall; garden court enclosed by tall screens. Panels of exposed aggregate paving inset in asphalt establish traffic patterns.*

### An entry and a carport

This landscape remodel achieved a new entry court and a new carport. As shown in the photographs here, the old carport required cars to negotiate a sharp turn within a few feet of the front door. This was hazardous for anyone on foot; also, this arrangement exposed large windows on this side of the house to full view from the street.

The problems were solved by shifting one wall of the carport, and putting in a new, wider driveway to the left of the old drive. Now cars move directly into the carport, and a generous entrance court and garden effectively screen the house from the street. A remaining portion of the old driveway provides a stall for guest parking.

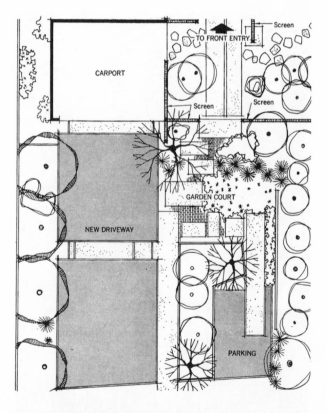

*BEFORE. Awkward turn required by car to reach carport. Turnaround occupied much of the level lot space.*

*NEW PLAN brings wider driveway directly into carport. Garden court, parking added. Design: Glen Hunt.*

## Streetside garden in the Japanese manner

This garden filled the owner's wish for a minimum maintenance garden. To add interest to the flat lot, mounds of earth were pushed up and the exposed subsoil covered with gravel.

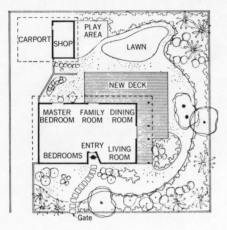

*PLAN shows fine development of small lot. Fence surrounds lot on three sides. Design: Edward M. Watanabe.*

*SCREENS of translucent plastic panels provide privacy for patio. Gate leads to driveway and garage.*

*ON STREETSIDE, garden is visible through 5½-foot, wire-on-wood-frame fence. Ample off-street parking provided. Gate opens to entrance footpath made of concrete rectangles.*

*TRELLIS-COVERED approach to front entrance extends and widens original driveway of random paving between street, carport. Free-standing screens are stained deep charcoal brown to blend with house.*

*BEFORE. Front door was narrow and uninviting; grove of madrones dwarfed the house. Glass wall faced street.*

## Screens and trellises make the difference

Wood screens and overhead trellises gave the front of this house a completely new character and provided the owners with needed privacy. Originally the front door looked like a back door and a floor-to-ceiling glass wall was in full view of the street. To create an attractive private entrance, every inch of the 16 feet available between house and driveway was used. Now you walk to the front door between and under a series of upright and overhead screens. The same screening also angles around an existing dogwood tree to enclose a 12 by 20-foot garden. In scale with the garden, screens are light in feeling, with 1 x 1-inch cedar members set vertically in 3-foot-wide panels. Screens and overhead structures are framed with cedar 2 x 4's.

OVERHEAD TRELLISES *match vertical screens, designed to support weight of wisteria vines. Pine in tub.*

SCREENED GARDEN, *12 feet wide, 20 feet long, seen through glass wall in hall. Plants lighted at night.*

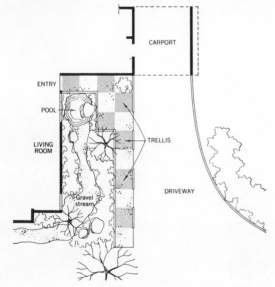

CARPORT

ENTRY

POOL

LIVING
ROOM

TRELLIS

DRIVEWAY

Gravel
stream

PLAN SHOWS *small, narrow garden. Dry stream bed carries off winter rain. Design: William G. Teufel.*

SHADE-TOLERANT *plants include Fatsia japonica, aucuba, bamboo, azaleas, ferns, rhododendrons, maple.*

*NEW FACADE created by fencing two sides of L formed by house and garage; relates garden to house.*

## Screened entries provide a new exterior look

The two houses on this page and the one on the facing page are good examples of combining house remodeling with new landscape design.

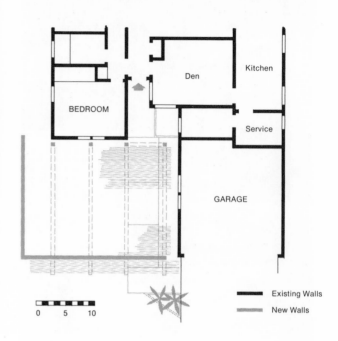

Legend:
- ▬ Existing Walls
- ▬ New Walls

*PLAN shows size of front garden and its relation to rooms. Design of three houses: Matlin and Dvoretsky.*

*SOLUTION: Shutters removed, wood screen added at entry. Planter extends porch line, lowers height of house.*

*BEFORE REMODELING, the house was undistinguished, too high in proportion to width.*

*NEW LINES and planes work together to emphasize horizontal, making house seem firmly planted on site. Patio wall, trellis extend lines of garage; slope terraced and planted to increase illusion of depth.*

*EXISTING HOUSE. Front yard unbroken slope. House looks boxy—no horizontal line to tie it together.*

*NEW BEDROOM PATIO screened from street and entry by walls of concrete block. The slope is terraced.*

## The garden gate and wall as part of the house

As glass walls in contemporary houses grow bigger and open more widely to enclosed gardens or entrance courts, garden walls begin to function as the outer walls of the house, and gates become doorways. These photographs make the case for relating wall, fence, and gate to the architecture of your house by using similar materials, colors, textures and design characteristics.

*GARDEN GATE has panel of ¾-inch plywood on reverse side to prevent sagging. Design: Robert W. Ramsey.*

*MASSIVE WOODEN GATES swing from wood strips bolted onto wall. Spanish motif of house reflected.*

*OPEN SCREEN fence with doorbell installed next to gate. Design: A. O. Bumgardner and Partners.*

*GALVANIZED steel pickets, painted black, set in frame form gate. Architects: Ian Mackinlay and Associates.*

## Some ideas for making your arrivals pleasant

The following photographs may give you some ideas for landscaping entries, that will give pleasant visual experiences to your guests.

*GENEROUS STEPS lead to entry terrace. Pine, Natal plum, geraniums flank walk. Design: Charles Darland.*

*NEAR STREETSIDE by path, cork oak, Natal plum, and native boulder make effective group.*

*NATURAL SCULPTURE, a piece of driftwood, provides focal point of interest. Display platform simple.*

*BAFFLE forms a background for low bench, glass jug, sweeping mass of Natal plum. Palms behind fence.*

**Additional ideas . . .**

CONIFERS *line entrance walk. Aleppo pine has been trained in an interesting form. Rock on ground.*

TINY SUCCULENTS *create mosaic of color, texture in bed with mailbox. Design: Armstrong & Sharfman.*

TAMARIX JUNIPERS *planted in streetside strip covered with decomposed granite. In bed, creeping juniper.*

JAPANESE BLACK PINE *stands next to red granite boulder near entrance. Design: Andre Cuenoud.*

ROADSIDE PARKING AREA *delineated by horizontal grapestake fence, concrete wall that supports change of grade. Monterey pines add vertical element. Woodwardia ferns, Cytisus canariensis inside fence.*

WAX-LEAF PRIVET *in pot near entry. Gravel used as ground cover; dwarf privet in back. Designer: Mel Harte.*

DRIVEWAY AND HOUSE *located to preserve maximum number of live oaks. Monterey pines on sides.*

## PLAY AREAS

If you turn loose a group of 5-year olds—boys and girls—on an acre of land where play places are a beautiful lawn, a cattle-loading chute, a full stand of tall grass and weeds, an old tree, a broken down truck, a pile of scrap lumber, a regulation jungle gym, where would you find them most of the time? Not in the places you prepared for them.

When you set aside a corner of a 60-foot lot and label it for "child play", the very best you can say for it is that it acknowledges that the children have rights to a place strictly their own. But if you are wise, you will allow for garden use beyond the sandbox, swings, and basketball hoop. Garden use by children will mean a different thing in each family. In some families, gardening and child raising are perfectly compatible. In other cases, the parent may prefer that the garden be all play space—at least while the children are little.

In the next few pages, and scattered throughout the book, you will find plans that have been developed with children in mind. Look at them with an eye to the complete space for play and the provision for change with changing interests.

*SPRING TOYS beside house are hidden from terrace. Toys are anchored in concrete for active use.*

*CHILDREN'S PLAY AREA is provided in the enclosed front garden. They can peek through to the street, ride trikes around raised beds without bumping or injuring the plants. Large paved area good for games.*

*RAISED BED serves as bench, protects plants from wheel toys. Angled screen directs view from family room to far end of garden. Covered patio contains space for warm-weather dining. Design: Mary Gordon.*

## They landscaped for children

Seven children and their friends use this subdivision garden as a play yard. Some of the children are still in the crawling or toddling stage so the owner wanted as much enclosed play space as possible without spoiling the garden for adults. The results work for both age groups.

In the front, lawn is reduced to a minimum between the sidewalk and a wall enclosing the larger part of the garden. Inside the wall, exposed aggregate paving provides running space for wheel toys, and two raised beds hold young flowering crab-apples which already give a show of spring flowers and will soon give summer shade as well. The tricycles can't bang into them, but going around is a good game. Creeping rosemary trailing over the brick withstands occasional crushing.

Bordering the pavement is dwarf lily-of-the-Nile, sold as variety 'Nana' or 'Peter Pan'. This perennial takes a certain amount of beating and needs very little care. Behind it are geranium and ivy geranium, a pyracantha, and ferns in a shady corner. Installed sprinklers supply water throughout the garden. The side yard is graveled, and given over to a playhouse and spring-mounted hobby "horses" (some have heads of other animals).

In the rear, exposed aggregate paving circles the lawn, which was installed in the shape of a pool in case the owners or future residents want one later.

Raised beds circle two sides (again a protection against wheel toys), and in them are planted two mature pines and an already mature hedge of glossy leaf privet.

These large plants were expensive, but they supplied an immediate screen that young plants would take years to duplicate. A collection of azaleas supplies spring color at the foot of the hedge. The large corner sandbox is screened from the house. In the bed below the screen are star jasmine and a *Daubentonia tripetii* that grows up onto the overhead and produces clusters of orange flowers in the summer.

*SANDBOX DECK continues line of raised beds. Screen, right, hides toys and sand from the patio area.*

*LANDSCAPING of rear garden on this 95-foot-wide lot was planned for children as well as adults. The large sandbox provides play space for the children in the family and their friends. Design: Gene K. Zema.*

### A private world for children

A garden in the midst of a pine forest is a most appealing place for children to play and adults to spend their leisure hours. That is the kind of garden the owners of the house pictured here wanted for their three young children and themselves. In these photographs you can see the charming, natural-looking garden that was created for them and the masterful way the plan is integrated with the house.

The dense plantings of Scotch pines and red oaks provide privacy and help confine the children's play activities to the paths and patio areas, at the same time giving the garden a feeling of spaciousness reminiscent of a forest clearing.

To encourage the trees to grow quickly, the areas of the garden where they were to be planted were excavated and refilled with topsoil, then planted with trees that averaged 5 feet in height. Three years later, they are 8 to 10 feet tall. The closely planted pines with dense branches clothed with sharp, stiff needles act as an effective barrier to keep the youngsters from wandering among the trees. A continuous fence behind the trees prevents them from venturing outside the garden.

As the pictures show, the contrasting textures of rocks, paving, sand, ground cover, shrubs, and trees add variety throughout the landscaped area.

A paved patio of unusually generous proportions fills much of the space between house and rear property line. A sandbox adjoining the patio gets intensive use in good weather. The sand drains rapidly after a heavy rain because drain tiles, installed 2 feet below the surface (and topped with heavy plastic film), carry the water away. The raised concrete firepit, placed in the angle of the bench, is also used as a base for a portable barbecue.

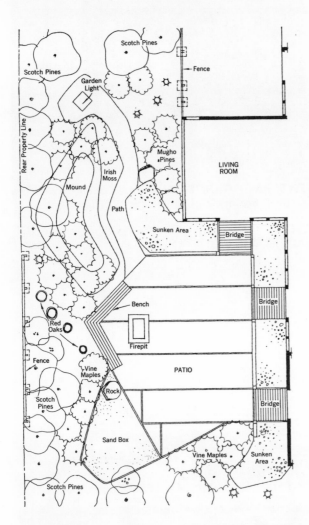

PLAN OF REAR GARDEN. *Simple and effective planting and large paved areas make this garden very livable.*

GREEN BANK *of Irish moss takes the normal wear and
tear of children at play. Moss is soft and springy.*

EXPOSED AGGREGATE *path, edged with Irish moss
and stones. Curves in path add interest, are natural.*

YOUNG LADIES *can go to any of several private nooks
in garden to exchange secrets, yet not get lost.*

## Garden for use of an active young family

The two photographs you see here show the first stage of a landscape plan intended for gradual, continued development. The garden was designed to be installed by the owners over several years, and still be of immediate use to an active, young family.

The 60-foot-wide, level lot has a great deal of outdoor living space: an entrance court, as well as a large back area of lawn, paving and flower beds. Future plans include adding an arbor, more fencing, and more shrubs. In the meantime, the garden is attractive and usable.

*ENTRANCE GARDEN kept simple. Color provided by seasonal accents. Design: Robert W. Chittock.*

*ROOFED TERRACE opens to living and family rooms, provides dry play area in rainy weather. In front is open terrace paved in long concrete ribbons. Annuals fill spaces. Paved area provides good tricycling area.*

*MERRY-GO-ROUND is fun for more than one. Base is cemented into ground. Design: Otis B. Renalds.*

*COMMUNITY SANDBOX is framed by railroad ties, two high; corners overlap. Design: Myron C. Lewis.*

*YOUNG ARTISTS can draw outdoors on this large board. Section of screen between carport and terrace was framed, with chalk trough at bottom, finished with blackboard paint. Design: Mrs. Robert K. Gordon.*

## LIVING AREAS

The planning of children's play areas and gardens to face the public have been discussed earlier in this chapter. Now, let us turn our attention to the areas in the garden that are for living—your outdoor living room. This may be all of your garden or only a small portion, but it must be livable and comfortable for you. The views you see must be pleasant and relaxing. Most all of the elements discussed in this book will come to play in planning and executing your outdoor living room. On the following pages are many examples which may give you further ideas.

### It's an entry, a patio, and a garden room

This enclosed area demonstrates an unusually attractive and functional indoor-outdoor relationship. Located between the family room and bedroom wing with the living-dining area in the rear, it serves both as an entry court and outdoor living room.

The expanded metal screen, added for aesthetic reasons, not for privacy, softens and adds a filagree-like design to the translucent glass wall of a hallway along the bedroom wing. The long horizontal lines of the screen, slightly curved to match a bench in front, increase the patio's apparent size and add a variety of feeling to the somewhat harsh rectangle. To filter the sun in the space open to the sky, an evergreen pear (*Pyrus kawakami*) was selected in preference to an architectural feature. The tree's greenness, texture, and varying shadow patterns offer a pleasant contrast to the rigidity of four walls, paving, and other structural elements. Star jasmine grows at the base of the tree.

The raised bed and planted corners help to break up the large paved surface. Sword fern, *Podocarpus gracilior*, clivia, and liriope are planted in the bed to the right of the living room door. Climbing fern asparagus (*A. plumosus*) makes a filmy tracery against the metal screen panel. A japonica camellia grows in a box on the left side of the door.

*ENTRY COURT at night. Guests find it inviting; owners enjoy its close relation to house. Design: Mary Gordon.*

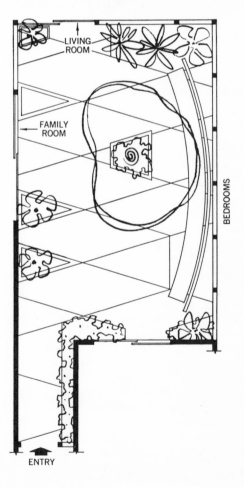

*DOUBLE-PURPOSE entry court, outdoor living room between wings of house. Plants add softness to paving.*

STREET VIEW. *From this angle you see part of the garden on the other side. In front of the brick wall ivy covers the ground, and pittosporum grows against the wall. Design: George E. Martin.*

## Two-faced garden

This front garden shows a trim, dignified face to the passer-by and a much different face—more colorful, more relaxed, and more relaxing—to anyone in the private area on the other side of the brick wall. The owners wanted a garden with a place for outdoor eating, relaxing, and entertaining in the front —on the south side, the side sheltered from summer winds. They wanted this outdoor living area to have privacy from the street. And they wanted the kind of streetside garden that they could most easily keep presentable.

You see from the street an always neat, clean combination of ground cover (English ivy), low hedge (*Pittosporum crassifolium*), brick wall, and wall rimmer (variegated Algerian ivy). It's a combination that requires little watering—once in the summer, if at all—and it always looks impeccably groomed because all the plants are so easy to care for. The owner squares off the sides of the bed of ivy and shears the hedge once every two months. Once a year he cuts back to the main stem the ivy on top of the wall.

You enter the inside garden around a baffle in the brick wall. There you see a much different sort of garden. The owners can relax in privacy on their patio (just off the front door) and enjoy an almost constantly colorful scene provided by camellias, carnations, daphne, hydrangeas, iris, and other plants.

VIEW FROM PATIO. *Patio provides area for outdoor living screened from street. Informality is theme.*

*MAIN OUTDOOR LIVING area is a paved terrace off family room, kitchen. Heating coil in paving gives about 30 additional days of outdoor living a year. Overhead provides shelter. Design: Robert Chittock.*

## Outdoors and indoors blend together

Good things can happen when architect and landscape architect work together through all stages of development from preliminary sketches to finished drawing. The house illustrated on these pages is the result of that kind of cooperation.

On their wooded, sloping lot, the owners wanted a house that would open out to the trees and the view to the southwest. They wanted, at the same time, to shut themselves off from the street. The house was designed and placed so that only four of the existing trees had to be removed. On the garden side they used a great deal of glass, and the living and sleeping areas of the house all look out on this side across

terraces into the garden. On the street side, a long brick wall runs across the width of the lot, opening only for the driveway. Even the carport is shielded from the street view. On the garden side, to make the terraces more useful in wet weather, the eaves form a deep overhang to shelter outdoor furniture on rainy days.

In the garden itself, the original woodsy feeling of the lot has been preserved as much as possible. Trees grow right on the terrace level, and the exposed aggregate paving of the terrace is carried out into the garden as lawn border, steps, and walks. Large rocks were brought in, and then were weathered by painting with a special mixture to promote moss growth.

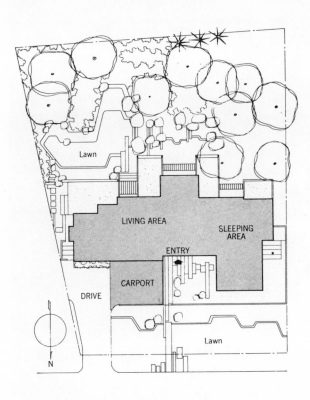

PLAN SHOWS *orientation of glass areas to southwest. Existing trees provide summer shade for the house.*

THREE TERRACES, *each terminated by a bench, are joined by bridges. Shaded areas invite outdoor games.*

CASTING *of concrete aggregate serves as bird bath, is the focal point of entry garden. Rocks cover ground.*

TRANSITION *from cultivated garden to woodsy slope is made by many interesting rock-plant combinations.*

*FLOOR-LEVEL DECK, reached through kitchen door beyond tree, creates a pleasant new garden space for sitting, entertaining. Bench along edge of deck provides seating. Design: Armstrong & Sharfman.*

## The deck makes this garden

It is usually difficult to create a pleasant garden when half the available space is taken up by a driveway and a detached garage. This small garden handles this situation unusually well. Its chief elements are a broad (24-foot-wide), low-level deck, fencing that screens off the driveway, and a design that keeps the space from seeming cramped.

*FENCE effectively screens view of driveway and garage from deck. Evergreen pear tree grows through deck well.*

*TWO-ELEMENT FENCE, gate separate garden from driveway. Curved lines emphasize illusion of distance.*

*CORNER of new deck is like an outdoor room, with enclosure on three sides, Mexican furniture and wrought iron candelabrum overhead. Asparagus ferns in hanging baskets add soft green color.*

## If one deck is good . . . why not another?

The pleasant front deck at the right suggested the way to improve the rear garden of this house. The back garden did have a brick patio, but the step down to it was awkward, the flat area was uninteresting, and the hillside dominated the view. The corner of the new deck is like an outdoor room and provides more outdoor living space.

*BROAD STEPS that repeat front deck design invite passage to private side patio for master bedroom.*

*EXISTING PRIVATE streetside deck off master bedroom has new bench-platform. Potted plants add color.*

# Remodeling an Established Garden

The urge to remodel an older garden strikes in various ways and for many reasons:

You buy a home that has been landscaped by a person who loved the very plants that you can very well get along without.

Or, after a three-year try, you look at your own handiwork and are sick of it. The shrub you thought would be gray-green is as lively as green grass. The shrubs that were supposed to remain low are covering the windows. The patio is too small and too hot.

Or you find yourself with an overgrown, 30-year-old garden, rich and lush in plant material but poor and cramped in living space.

Or the family is growing up. Tricycles have changed to bicycles; you need a basketball court instead of a sandbox.

Don't resist reasonable urges to change. Even changing just for the sake of change has its rewards. It is one of the ways you can enjoy the satisfactions that come with being a designer—the refreshment to the eye, the sense of creating something beautiful, the new ability to see the form and texture of plants.

To exercise your designing eye, drive through a street of pleasant homes and look at the streetside planting of each with the question, "Would I choose this as an example of a good planting arrangement?" Most plantings would be too spotty, too jumpy. Some would be too sparse; many would be overgrown. After looking at a hundred gardens, you might be ready to re-examine your own with fresh eyes. Often as not, then will come the urge to remodel your own garden.

*COMFORTABLE bench of cedar boards (stained brown) has sloped backrest. More about this garden on page 91. Design: Chaffee-Zumwalt & Associates.*

## DOING OVER THE MATURE GARDEN

If you are living with a garden someone else planted 15 or 30 years ago and it does not satisfy you, you very likely face a drastic job of garden remodeling. Is this older garden your master or your servant? Does it tax your time and budget to keep it up? Does it give you the space you want for outdoor entertaining, for sun-bathing, for growing the plants you want to grow?

The charm of many an old garden is in its overgrown foliage, its sheltered pools of deep shade. Little by little over the years, the domestic jungle closes in, and without anyone's quite knowing when it happens, the garden no longer has a place for sun-loving flowers, and the service yard has no place for drying clothes. Even indoor living suffers; foundation planting has overgrown the windows, blotting out the sun.

When you study the planting in such a garden, you often find in the mixture of shrubs and trees many that were originally planted for quick effects or were selected without thought of eventual size. Woody plants grow higher when treated as trees than when allowed to grow as shrubs. With energies diverted into a single upward channel, a plant that has remained 12 feet high as a mature shrub may reach 20 feet as a tree. By training old shrubs as trees, you can relieve congestion and gain new planting space around the base. You also improve them in health and appearance.

Plants in any older garden may gradually shade the windows of a house until finally most of the sun is cut off. Pruning, rearranging, and adding plants will get pleasant results.

So the first step in remodeling an overgrown garden is to move in with saw and pruning shears. Clear away enough of the excess growth to see what you have. Next, thin out the overhead canopy. Most old trees will benefit from thinning; the shafts of sunlight that penetrate will give the undergrowth a chance to develop. These thinning and clearing operations should allow you to see and appraise the basic frame of your garden.

If you are remodeling an old garden to get play space for children, don't overlook its special opportunities for tree house, "camp" sites, hideouts. A private, overgrown path leading nowhere can give as many hours of pleasure to children as a jungle gym. For other ideas, see pages 72 through 77.

## REMODELING FOR EASIER MAINTENANCE

Many older gardens were designed for regular maintenance by a hired gardener. Today, with garden help both scarce and expensive, these gardens present a formidable maintenance problem. Even with the help of power mowers, electric hedge clippers, and wheeled fertilizer spreaders, the garden simply takes up too much of the owner's time.

The first step in remodeling your garden for easier maintenance is to take a close look at your over-all plan. In many older gardens, the plan is a formal one. Highly symmetrical plans usually call for meticulous edging. The great variety in plant material makes maintenance difficult. There may be edges to trim, lawn borders to clip, annual beds to cultivate and change, and individual specimens to shape and care for.

Simplifying, arranging mass groupings of plant material, confining lawn and plant beds with header boards, using ground covers and pavings, and building raised beds will all result in lower maintenance. For details, see pages 44 through 55. The photographs on this page illustrate one solution.

*COMFORTABLE DECK provides level outdoor living space on sloping lot. The view is captured from here.*

*PATH from side garden joins deck near a corner of the house. Zig-zag rail follows the brow of the hill.*

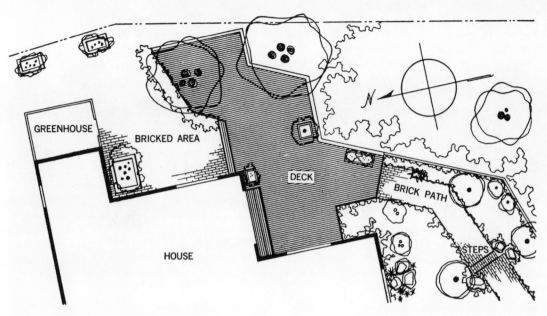

PLAN SHOWS irregular shape of lot with house occupying two-thirds of ground space. Formal garden re-placed by simplified planting. Deck for level living space. Design: Carol Wieting.

LEAN-TO greenhouse at rear is surrounded by brick paving; it houses a sizable collection of hibiscus.

COLLECTION of small shrubs grows in garden now. Plants chosen for all-season effectiveness, ease of care.

TWO NEW DECKS, *oriented to catch maximum sun and take advantage of view, project from house at living room level. Sturdy supports and rails reflect feeling of house, and are stained redwood like the house.*

VISTA *along path leading from carport around deck to play court and garden. Design: Glen Hunt & Associates.*

## REMODELING FOR OUTDOOR LIVING

Having more than enough garden to maintain, yet no usable space for outdoor living, is a fairly common problem. The photographs shown on these two pages illustrate a solution.

The remodeling includes a large deck easily reached from the house and placed to get as much sun as possible, a paved game court, and a garden designed for minimum maintenance.

The result is a garden but no lawn; the grass was replaced with gravel, paving, and decking. Shrubs and flowers are in raised beds. On the paved game court, basketball, badminton, paddle tennis, and tetherball can be played. The children can skate and ride bikes there, too.

BEFORE *remodeling, shaded lawn was wet underfoot; level living space was limited. Existing deck small.*

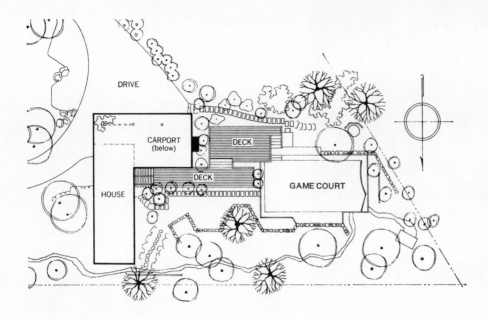

PLOT PLAN *shows relation of the house to decks, game court. Note screen of native trees on north and west boundaries. Steps of the deck serve as a seating area for game court spectators.*

GAME COURT AND DECK *cover most of open space where lawn used to be. Concrete pillars support deck. Generous rectangular concrete pads in gravel carry foot traffic around north side of house to court.*

*FENCE AND GATE stained dark brown to blend with shingle siding on house. Light for night safety.*

## On a hillside

Here is another garden that was remodeled to gain more outdoor living space. The problem was presented by having the living and dining rooms facing the front. Because of this arrangement and the fact that the house is on a hill and covers most of the lot, a patio off the front was the only reasonable solution. Along with the outdoor remodeling, sliding glass doors were installed to make the patio accessible from the living and dining rooms.

The garden was remodeled six years before these photographs were taken. It has matured well, and now blends with the older house.

*STEEPEST PART of bank planted with rockrose, ceanothus below. Design: Eckbo, Dean & Williams.*

*BEFORE, no outdoor living here unless you sat on covered porch. Windows by car belong to dining room.*

*NEW PATIO, screened from street by fence (behind camera), shaded from afternoon sun by house. New sliding doors, steps allow easy access to dining room at right. Living room is at the left.*

## More level living space

Another example of a garden that was remodeled to obtain outdoor living space that was level and private is illustrated on this page. This scheme provides deck and terrace space level with the main floor of the house. The narrow walk from the garage to the house was replaced by a paved terrace sheltered by overhead trellises and screens for privacy from the street and the houses higher on the hill.

The deck, built over the garden, adjoins the paved terrace and contains a comfortable bench. The closeness of the terrace and deck to the kitchen makes outdoor dining convenient.

*OVERHEAD TRELLIS and screen fence, stained dark brown, add to privacy of terrace and deck.*

*BENCH serves as railing for deck. It provides comfortable seating for view of the garden.*

*PAVED TERRACE, deck join. In this view, garage entrance shown at top of page is to right. Continuation of entrance trellis will mask garage wall when vines get older. Design: Chaffee-Zumwalt & Associates.*

*NEW DECK, connected with living room by a slightly sloping ramp, seems part of the house. It extends across the entire rear wall of the house and is framed by a variety of plants.*

*BEFORE. Living room windows and door faced the yard used mainly as a playground by the children.*

## REMODELING WITH DECKS AND TERRACES

The addition of a simple deck demonstrates once again how easy it is to make a garden more usable. Adding a deck to the house illustrated in the photographs on this page made it easier for the owners to walk out into the garden and see their plants up close. It provided a place for outdoor visiting, eating and children's games. And, of course, it transformed the look of both house and garden.

Before the deck was added (photograph at left), the garden consisted of a larger, level lawn with a border of miscellaneous shrubs and perennials. Now the lawn curves in and out following the lines of the deck.

The addition of the spacious deck to the house shown in the photographs on the opposite page results in the better use of the outdoor area. The appearance of the house is vastly improved, and the adjoining family room appears much larger.

DECK, 12 feet wide, is accessible from family room (left), and the balcony leading to front door.

BEFORE. Photograph shows west end of house before the addition of the deck and carport.

DECK ADDITION forms roof for carport, adds large, convenient outdoor living room, and improves the exterior appearance of this house. Screens give needed privacy from street. Design: Glen Hunt.

*LIVING-DINING room opens to outdoor room. Deck, at floor level for easy passage in and out through sliding glass door, is partially shaded by overhead trellis. Design: Matlin & Dvoretzky, Warren Waltz.*

*BEFORE remodeling, house had conventional windows, hinged door, and 2-foot step down to small patio.*

## A deck that wraps around the house

When there is a change of level between the house and garden, a deck often will provide an easy, attractive way to move between the two. Here is an example:

By remodeling only on the outside, around all four sides, the livability of this house was increased enormously. The only changes that affected the inside were in windows and doors. A floor level deck crosses the entire rear of the house and wraps around into each side yard. In front, in the entry garden, a similar deck expands the former skimpy front porch and links it with a new sliding glass door to the master bedroom.

Before, there were three doors to the outside. Now five rooms (including the two front bedrooms) open at floor level to a deck. This improved access in and out has altered the way the interior of the house works, so in effect the interior has been remodeled without the knocking down of any walls.

NEW ENTRY is at left; extended front wall creates entry behind. The front windows, now narrower, are louvered. Master bedroom has view of entry garden. Entrance made more inviting.

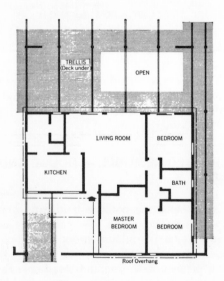

FLOOR PLAN. The rear remodeling added more than 700 square feet of usable living area.

BEFORE. Conventional subdivision house, L-shaped, bedrooms in front. Garage at rear off of an alley.

## REMODELING TO GET MORE PRIVATE SPACE

Many old garden layouts gave generously "to the public." The more exclusive the neighborhood, the greater the setback. With garden labor and water prices what they are, keeping up a front area that you can't use in any way becomes a costly burden.

The simplest way to get privacy is to build a 6-foot fence at the setback line. If this type of fencing is incompatible with your garden, your neighborhood, or your city ordinances, you can grow a dense screen with plant material. Vines on a trellis or a wire-filled frame will also give you privacy. (See pages 57 through 71 for entry garden ideas in gardens with deep setbacks.)

You may want to remodel your front garden for offstreet parking. Chances are that many more cars park on your street today than parked there when your garden was planned; this can offer real problems, not only for your guests but for the car (or cars) in your family. To gain the needed space, a deep setback now devoted to lawn can be reshaped and partially paved. Planting can screen cars from the street and/or from the house.

Remember these points when you plan for off-street parking:

• Choose a convenient spot for your own car, preferably only a short walk from the door.

• Make it simple for your guests to park. You might indicate car spaces by changes in pavement material, flush header boards, or built-up dividers and bumper strips.

• Make it possible for any guest to leave easily at any time. If the cars have to be packed bumper to bumper, a wholesale car-moving is necessary if one person wants to leave early.

• Don't skimp on the minimum provisions indicated in the sketches below. Try to keep all traffic headed forward—as a rule, no guest likes to back out of an unfamiliar driveway or parking area.

Even though garages or parking lots with attendants may use less space, your plans for parallel, diagonal, and vertical parking should stick to the recommended minimums as diagrammed below and to the right.

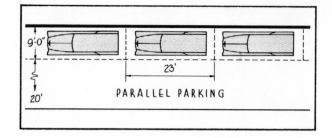

PARALLEL PARKING

The illustration below indicates the minimum requirements for the turnaround if the car is to be backed out of the garage or carport. (Allow more space if it is to be backed in.) The broken lines indicate the back wheel tracks, and the solid lines the front wheel tracks. Note the added 3 feet necessary for turning.

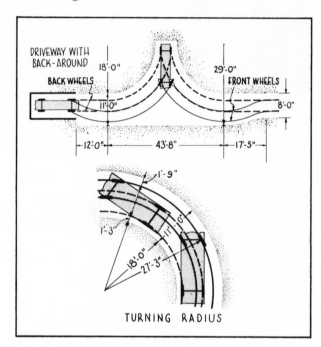

TURNING RADIUS

Add 10 feet to the outside of the turning radius if you want to park cars on the turn. Front and back wheels do not follow each other precisely when the car is making a sharp turn.

## COORDINATED REMODEL — HOUSE AND GARDEN

Often the best starting point in landscape remodeling is the house itself. The new patio may work a lot better if you step outdoors through a sliding glass door, as illustrated in several of the houses on the preceding pages and throughout this book. Removing an old porch and building a generous deck in its place can change the entire character of your garden. See the following pages for examples.

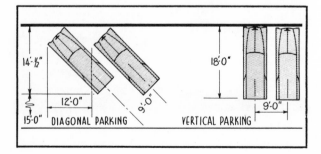

DIAGONAL PARKING     VERTICAL PARKING

## A new glass wall and a deck

The plans for remodeling the house called for moving the front door to one end of the house and creating an entry hall with a much needed coat closet. The living room was then opened out through large windows and a pair of doors to a new floor-level deck and a view into the thickly planted parking strip. The roofline was not changed, but the covered porch was removed.

The remodeling of this older home for more usable living space in the front of the house was made possible by a deep setback and a wide strip of trees and shrubs screening the house and garden from view of the street.

*BEFORE. This was the front entry. You walked directly into living room. No outdoor living area.*

*BRIDGE takes you to new entry at end of the house. Living room, deck hidden by screen.*

*GARDEN now is just outside living room, and there is a bridge-deck for sitting. Behind camera, entry path winds up through thickly wooded area to street, guest parking area. Design: A. O. Bumgardner.*

*ADULTS' TERRACE made by creating two paved levels. Play yard behind screen, upper right. Upper level shaded by overhead trellis. Planting softens large paved areas. Landscape design: Roberta Wightman.*

## One new room . . . two new terraces

When either modernizing or adding a room to your house, you may want to think of a landscape remodel as a basic part of the total job. By coordinating the two, both house and garden might benefit, as shown by the photographs on this page. Here the back porch became a breakfast room and indoor play area, and the outdoor area was made both a children's play yard and a terrace and patio for adults.

*ENCLOSED PORCH now indoor play, dining area. Play area visible through windows. Design: William Bain, Jr.*

*BEFORE REMODELING, photograph shows roofed, open porch at right, old entry deck, sloping front lawn.*

## A garden terrace

The following photographs illustrate another example of coordinated house and garden remodeling. The porch and stairs were added when the kitchen at the rear of the house was remodeled. The large oblong concrete stones were set in gravel to provide firm footing for outdoor furniture.

*BEFORE remodeling, the kitchen door opened out to a flight of steps leading into the garden.*

*NATIVE OAKS, greens (as in bed of oxalis) are important in garden. Dwarf bamboo in containers on porch.*

*PORCH OFF BREAKFAST ROOM, terrace below. Glass doors removed for openness in warm weather. Porch is supported on posts resting on granite blocks. Similar rocks in garden. Design: Kaye Scott.*

## An outdoor floor

In this situation, the deep setback from the street suggested a private garden off the master bedroom in front. On the south side, the rear garden could hold a pool.

Now, floor-level decks make it easy to move in and out to a new garden room and to the rear garden. Fencing across the front creates a private bedroom garden and unifies the facade. New sliding glass doors open up the master bedroom and living, dining, and breakfast rooms to the outdoors. Vine trellises shelter the entry, garden room, and part of the rear deck and terrace. The new outdoor areas enlarge the house's usable space—and add the amenity that was missing.

*Caution:* Before starting any construction job that is connected in any way with existing buildings—house, garage, lath structure, etc.—have all foundations inspected. If you go ahead without knowing the exact condition of existing structures, you may find yourself in trouble with the new ones.

If you live in an incorporated area, check with the building inspector to learn what can and what can't be built without a permit. In some cities, all structures (carports, lathhouses, fences, overheads, garden houses) must be approved in the plan stage.

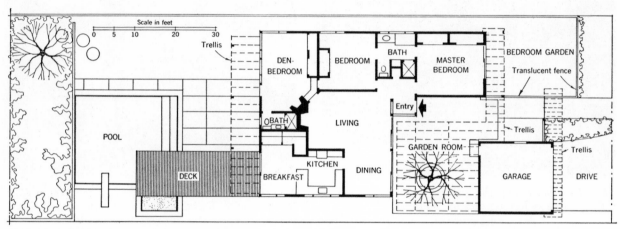

*FLOOR AND PLOT PLAN shows new deck areas near bedroom, dining room and pool. Every major room now has a garden view. Garden room created in front by entry gate and fence. Design: Alfred T. Wilkes.*

*IN FRONT, living and dining room floor plane flows into garden room created by the broad new deck, trellis, entry gate and fence, and the rear wall of the garage. Shade from tree and overhead.*

LARGE SLIDING GLASS DOOR *opens out onto expansive new deck. This door replaces former small window and makes the interior rooms seem much larger. Kitchen also shares this breakfast-room view.*

BEFORE. *Detached garage, in front of L-shaped house. Existing courtyard not exploited. Small windows.*

AFTER. *Trellis, fencing tie garage into unified facade. Translucent plastic fence creates needed privacy.*

# Plans for Hillsides and Sloping Lots

In this discussion of ways to landscape a hillside, we accept all sloping sites as hillsides. The site may be anything from a natural slope with a fall of only 4 feet in 100, to a carved out "bench" with a sudden sheer drop in front and a high cut bank in back.

Every slope is a different landscaping problem, but all slopes have features in common. When the bulldozer made it possible to grade out a level lot almost anywhere, most hillside home sites changed from slopes to a series of benches. The bulldozer did much the same kind of a job on the hillside sites for individually built homes as it did in the subdivision, except that in the subdivision it carved the bench pads in series. The result: a great variety of hillside situations. Some have a short level lot with a bank sloping down in front and up in back or vice versa; some have a narrow level space with an up-bank on one side and a down-bank on the other; some have variations in two-way slopes; some have natural slopes.

To get at solutions which would apply to each group, we have gathered together in the following pages examples of several types of hillside landscaping. If you study these plans, you'll see that the sloping site offers many opportunities for imaginative planning in outdoor living and gardening.

A well planted steep bank can become the backdrop of your own private garden amphitheater. A hillside with a 12-foot rise, planted with shrubs and ground cover, gives a house as much privacy and wind protection as does a line of 5-year old trees.

A two-level garden offers mystery and surprise as you move up and down. A planting of trees on the lower level can blot out a view of roof tops and often convert a commonplace view into a panorama.

*BRICK PADS alternate with concrete steps that provide display space for potted plants. Ivy and junipers cover slope. More about garden on pages 106 and 107.*

If your slope faces south, you can enjoy growing many more tender or heat-loving plants than the gardener down on the flat. South slopes warm up earlier in the year and receive more total sunshine. Cold air flows downhill, leaving you from 5 to 10° warmer than the cold pockets below you.

Hillside topsoils are usually thinner than the soils of valleys, but you can concentrate your good soil in the terraces needed in most hillside gardens.

There are, of course, some inherent problems. Hillside gardening means drainage and grading problems—water flows downhill and water erodes. It means digging out or building up for a level patio. It means putting in steps or ramps from one level to another. In short, the sloping site demands more thought, more work, and sometimes more expense.

## MODERATELY SLOPING SITE

Following the contour—stringing the house out along the face of the slope—is a favorite design technique of architects and homeowners who want the house to fit into its site with a minimum of fuss.

Shallow slopes pose fewer problems in landscaping for outdoor living, because patios or terraces can go on one side or the other of the house. The long line of the structure seldom permits floor level terraces at either end, sometimes the only choice on a steeply sloping site.

On a moderately sloping site, you have a choice: Use the most level ground for the house and project floor-level decks for outdoor living areas. Or build the house out over the slope and use the level land for patios, terraces, or garden.

The house shown on the next page combines a bit of both. It joins the land where the grade is most level, and floats over the slope where it isn't. The floor-level deck extends the rooms outside. The house fits the site, and since there was little altering of the natural grade, erosion and drainage problems are minimized.

*REFLECTING POOL and decked sitting area are off the dining room. Beyond screens is patio off the kitchen and a bedroom, also a level lawn and garden. Landscape architects: Chaffee-Zumwalt & Associates.*

*DECK off living room has view, also functions as roof for carport. Steps up to the entry are hidden behind the pine, bamboo grove. As plants grow, the house will seem to be more wedded to site.*

*VIEW FROM THE BACK of lot looks down into play area. The concrete retaining wall serves for handball.*

## TWO-WAY SLOPE

The house and garden on this page were designed to exploit the slope for a two-level garden. So this new house would fit into its older, established neighborhood a fairly formal, tailored streetside garden was designed. The back garden is divided into two major levels. The upper level off the family-dining room was kept simple and restrained; the lower level outside a basement room was designed as a play area for the entire family.

Although the lower play area seems complete and permanent just as it is, it has received a temporary treatment to last only until the small children grow up and a swimming pool can be fully used. The area where the pool will go is partly covered with a 1-inch skin of well-reinforced concrete to serve as a basketball court and a graveled area for swings and slides.

*PLAN SPECIFIES the location of the future swimming pool. Gravel can be swept aside and concrete removed.*

*UPPER LEVEL made private from play area by grade. Fence, rails repeat detail. Design: Robert Chittock.*

*FROM the street, doorstep is about at eye level. Entry walk is a progression of planes, edged with boulders and softened by plantings. Large native oaks shade steps. Design: Eriksson, Peters & Thoms.*

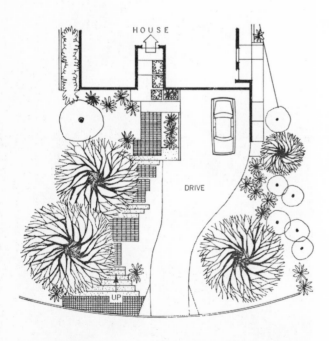

*GROUND PLAN shows new walk placed beside existing drive to carport. Note relation of steps to driveway.*

## STEEP FRONT AND BACK SLOPES

The greatest assets of the garden shown here posed its greatest problem. The assets are the steep slope up from the street, and two large, native oak trees. The problem: the slope made possible a dramatic garden composition—yet on one side, it could not be altered without damage to the trees.

In the remodeling, the main design feature was an indirect pathway under the oaks, up the slope but wide enough that it emphasized the horizontal rather than the vertical. New plantings completed the conversion from front yard to garden.

The garden in back of the house was carved from another slope, so steep that it had defeated all previous attempts to make it usable. Remodeling involved excavating and hauling away nine truckloads of soil, to shape a series of planes climbing to a sun deck platform. The design provided for large areas of paving—an initial expense that pays off in reduced maintenance requirements. The expanses of concrete are foreshortened and unobtrusive when viewed from the level of the lower patio. The sculptured slopes are held by a fine textured ground cover while a small dichondra lawn occupies part of the lower patio space.

VIEW FROM LIVING ROOM *toward rear deck. Three-level garden has large areas of paving, ground cover for easy maintenance. Steps provide display space for potted plants.*

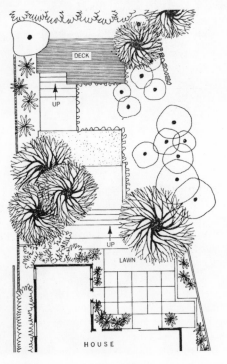

PLAN *shows the relation of the house to the rear garden. Fence lines the edge of the property.*

AT REAR OF GARDEN, *deck is an inviting place for sunning. Level areas provide outdoor living space.*

VIEWED *from living room window, middle elevation appears as island in landscaping and native trees.*

## DECKS DOWN THE HILLSIDE

When the owners of this home decided to build an outdoor living area, they didn't want to deface their carefully preserved, naturally wooded slope. Moreover, the presence of a septic tank and drain field on the bank ruled out any major concrete terrace work. As a result, they decided on decking—not one deck but three, at different elevations descending the slope.

The decks offer a variety of places to enjoy the outdoors. Separated by islands of landscaping, they are in harmony with the wooded surroundings. The installation of the decks required minimum site disturbance, so the structure runs little risk of washout; the bank's runoff is hardly altered. The decks were built around existing trees; none was removed.

The multiple decks don't have the costly under structure a single high deck would have needed (although the saving was partly offset by the cost of the steps).

MIDDLE DECK *has a different atmosphere. Here you look back toward steps bordered with rhododendrons, vine maple, and bamboo. Steps connect with the first level. Design: William G. Teufel.*

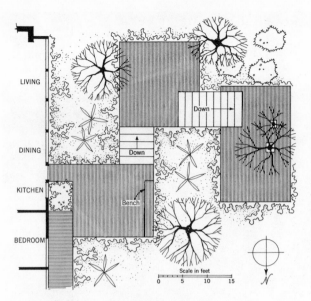

PLOT PLAN for three-deck outdoor living area. Each deck is shown in the photographs on these pages.

LOWEST DECK forms low arm of U plan. Native conifers border its down-slope side.

HIGHEST DECK is level with the house. Large expanses of glass open the house to decks and woodsy landscape. Straight ahead in this view are steps to next lower level. Plants and decks blend together.

*VIEW OF SIDE GARDEN. The deck at right is off living room; steps leading down to carport and entry at street level are edged with rhododendrons, heather, juniper, clematis. Design: Mr. & Mrs. James Hussey.*

*STEPS lead to small greenhouse. Plants include lush vancouveria, viburnum, ferns, vinca, fuchsias.*

## STEEP FRONT SLOPE

The garden pictured here was difficult to develop, but the efforts as shown in the photographs seem worth it. Topsoil was hauled up from the street in buckets to fill the beds that were outlined with logs and rock. Temporary retaining walls of shingles were made around some plants to keep them from washing out in the rain. Though massed planting and lawns are absent, this garden on a hillside brings plants up close where you can really see and enjoy them. Trailing plants show off better when they are allowed to spill down over the face of a log or stone retaining wall. And the jobs of weeding, nipping off faded flowers, and shaping and pruning are made much easier when many of the plants are within easy reach from hillside paths, steps, and decks.

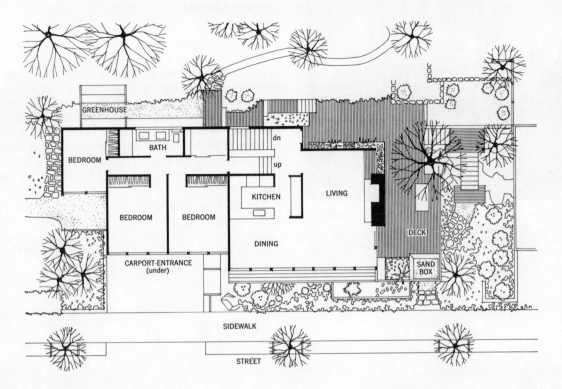

PLAN *shows the location of steps, deck, planting beds. The narrow area has been used for level living space and play areas.*

DOOR *ahead takes one into the living room from deck. Easy passage provided for foot traffic between garden, deck and house. The overhead protects white camellias from rain.*

BELOW-DECK *receptacle hides controls for sprinkling systems. Design: Chaffee-Zumwalt & Associates.*

## DECK GARDEN

This deck complex was designed to provide outdoor living areas for a family with small children. The house is perched on a steep hillside. The deck as shown in the photographs on these pages is full of surprises. Trees grow through the center, vine maple grows in a large concrete container, waterfalls spill from pool to pool, and there is a small circular scrap of lawn. The deck structure itself performs a variety of hidden storage functions; trapdoors lead to recessed boxes that hold hoses and sprinkler and fountain controls.

The deck has the effect of a hanging garden with bamboo, pine and *Fatsia* growing through the center.

DECK, *above steeply sloping hillside, provides space for the children to play, adults to entertain and garden. It features grass, trees, pools, and a view of Puget Sound.*

SUPPORTS *for the deck are braced wood uprights on concrete piers. Looking down, one can see trees on slope.*

HOSE *and water connections are concealed in this recessed box. This keeps clutter off the deck.*

TRAP DOOR *flush with deck lifts to reveal stairway to ground level. It's too heavy for youngsters to open.*

WATER *falls from cantilevered pool to a second pool, then splashes to still another pool on the ground.*

## GARDEN STEPS

Garden steps can be designed to fit almost any change of grade, but it is a good idea—for reasons of both convenience and safety—to stay close to a fairly standard riser-tread ratio. (The riser is the vertical portion of the step, determining how high you have to lift your foot; the tread is the horizontal portion, providing the surface on which you step.)

A good formula to approximate is a 6-inch riser and a 15-inch tread. Don't make the steps too narrow; 4 feet is a minimum width for two-abreast walking. On steep slopes it is better to break up a flight of steps with a landing or a change of direction rather than to settle for an awkward and possibly dangerous riser-tread ratio.

*WOODEN STEPS blend with woodland path and surrounding area. Another playmate is about to appear.*

*RAILROAD TIES set into bank and backed by gravel make rustic wide steps between lawn and woods.*

*SEVERITY of granite steps broken by planting over the rocks edging them. Tiny crocus peak through.*

BRICK RISERS *set in concrete in gravel to make walking across slope of lawn easier, and to keep feet dry.*

SPLIT CEDAR *rails, pegged into slope and edged with cedar rounds, facilitate traffic, blend into setting.*

STEEP DESCENT *is made less arduous by landings and offsetting steps. Plants soften stiffness of steps.*

STONE STEPS *all but hidden by creeping thyme, arabis, alyssum. Pocket plantings provide surprise and color.*

# Your Garden as an Outdoor Room

To provide a pleasant outdoor living room necessitates three of the same basic elements required for a room in your house—walls, floor, and ceiling. In addition, other factors can add to the livable hours that can be spent there; heat to chase away the chill of the night air, water to cool the hot afternoons.

In this chapter we have presented as completely as possible all the materials that can be used for floors, garden screens, and overhead shelter. There are ideas for combining these materials to create interest as well as to stretch your dollars. You will also find ideas for heating your patio and for the use of water for cooling.

## THE GARDEN FLOOR

Every outdoor flooring material has its limitations. But each has a place where it serves better in some way than any other material.

You cannot base your selection on one value alone if you intend to satisfy your eyes, your needs, your sense of fitness, and your budget.

Keep in mind the basic idea of your garden plan when you think about garden floor coverings. If you wish to create a mood of a woodsy retreat, slick concrete would be an intrusion. Wood blocks would be more suitable. Or tree rounds. Or stone. If you want the garden to take care of dancing parties and a shuffleboard court, concrete of the slickest finish is in order. If there are children and wheeled toys, the surface can't be too soft and it shouldn't have a knee-scratching roughness or a skull-splitting hardness. If one of the purposes of the garden is to invite the sun for outdoor living, a pavement of bricks, concrete, or asphalt will husband the warmth of the sun.

*OUTDOOR LIVING ROOM. Deck is really extension of living room, seen at right through wall of tall windows. Design: Robert Chittock.*

If you have too much sun, such pavings might only make your problem worse.

Whether you do the labor or hire the work done will influence your choice of materials. Many home owners prefer brick to concrete because bricks can be handled in a leisurely way.

Your selection need not be one material against the field. Combinations of two materials are often more attractive than one used alone. Amateurs and landscape architects before you have worked out variation upon variation. Many of the photographs in this book show effective combinations.

Let's look at the various paving materials.

## Bricks

Bricks as garden paving are handsome in almost any situation you can think of, from the curved sweep of an inviting patio to the straight pathways of a formal garden. And today you can choose a brick texture from rough to almost tile-smooth, a color from ebony to off-white. You can be an utter novice and still find bricklaying a challenge that needn't surpass your skill.

Of the two basic kinds of brick, common and face, common bricks are most used by home craftsmen and are less expensive . You can choose between sand mold and wire cut common, or their hard-fired varieties called clinkers.

The basic form and composition of brick has continued without much change for about 5,000 years. Heavy clay soil and water are mixed, molded or cut into blocks, and then baked (fired) in a kiln. In the standard brick the length is two widths plus a ½-inch mortar joint, or three thicknesses plus two mortar joints. Properly fired brick is hard enough to last for centuries and show only minor wear.

Most garden paving is done with common bricks. People like their familiar color and texture, and also their lower price. Face bricks are not as widely available as the common, and in the past they have been

*BRICK PATH set in half basket weave with headers placed so no bricks needed cutting. Ice plant contrasts.*

used mostly for facing walls and buildings. It is only recently that they have begun to be used to any degree in garden paving.

Face bricks are more durable and more uniform in color and size. (Common bricks may vary as much as ¼-inch in length.) They are less porous than common bricks and therefore will not absorb as much water.

Used brick, taken from old buildings and walls, is usually in short supply, and although it is not used much for paving an entire area, it can add a rustic look if set sparingly. To supplement the low supply of used brick, manufacturers convert new bricks to used by chipping them and splashing them with mortar and paint. Manufactured used bricks are not hard to find; they cost the same as the genuine ones.

The exact dimensions of a standard brick (both common and face) vary from region to region, and manufacturer to manufacturer. In the West, standard dimensions are about 2½ by 3¾ by 8 inches.

Today, there are many units larger and smaller than this that are excellent for paving. Among the most popular and readily available of these are the Norman, Roman, Split, and Split Paver.

Traditionally, the color of brick has been the color of the clay in the area where it is made; usually a red or red-brown. These are still the most popular, but the color range of brick has widened greatly over the years. Today, you can pave your garden with clay brick in tones of ebony, buff, carnation, red, and off-white.

Brick prices vary from area to area ranging from 6-20 cents or more a brick. When you order, ask about delivery charges; they are usually low, but often not included in the quoted price. It is a good idea to pay a little extra and have the bricks delivered on a pallet; this prevents what can be considerable breakage in unloading.

**Paving with bricks:** Brick looks well almost anywhere you want to put it, but there are two important things to consider before you start paving. Water must drain away from the area you pave, since shifting and problems with efflorescence can result if the water is allowed to stand under the bricks. If drainage is unusually poor, consider seeking professional help to correct it.

In choosing the bond or pattern you are going to make with your bricks, keep in mind the degree of difficulty involved. Some bonds can demand a good bit of accuracy and brick cutting.

Preparing the base is the most crucial task. No matter how carefully and assiduously you set bricks, if the base settles or shifts, you may have to begin all over again.

Start by setting up headers (a framework usually made of 1 by 4's or 2 by 4's, or doubled ¼ by 3's or ¼ by 4's for curves around the entire area you intend to pave).

Once you have framed the area, divide it with temporary headers into sections no more than 6 feet wide (the sections can run the length of the area). For example, an area 20 feet by 20 feet could be divided every 5 feet with temporary headers to make sections 20 feet long and 5 feet wide. When you begin to set the bricks, it is easier to keep them even in such a limited area. Once you have laid one strip, the header can be moved over for the paving of the next 5 feet.

When the headers are in place, turn over the soil and pulverize it, then screed (level) it. For adequate drainage (away from buildings, for example), grade it so that it slopes at least 1 inch every 6 feet, then tamp or roll it until the surface is hard and flat.

**Setting bricks on sand** is the easiest project for the beginner. Unless you live where the ground freezes, bricks in sand are fully as permanent (if you want them to be) and as durable as bricks that are set in mortar.

Spread sand to a depth of 1 to 2 inches between the headers. Now, wet the sand moderately to help it settle. With a screed (a 2 by 4 that rides on the headers with an extension that reaches down to the level of the sand), level the sand for about 3 feet between the headers. Lay the bricks in the pattern you have chosen, and tap them into place with a rubber mallet. Use a spirit level often to make sure the bricks are on the level you want. Now screed the next 3 feet, and repeat the process until all the bricks are in place.

Use fine sand (such as 30-mesh) between the bricks. Throw handfuls out across the top of the bricks and let dry in the sun for a few hours, then sweep it into the cracks. Repeat until the joints are filled; then wet the area with a light spray so that the sand between the cracks will settle completely.

**Paving over existing concrete:** If you are using face bricks, you will be able to seal them. Several acrylic sealers now on the market will work well on brick that is not too porous. The sealing will cut down efflorescence and help bind the sand in the joints. Common brick is usually much too porous to seal effectively.

If you have a concrete path or patio that you are tired of looking at, it is an easy matter to pave over it with bricks. For such projects, where the brick needs no thickness for stability, a standard split or split paver is best. Set up headers around the concrete. Spread about ½ inch of mortar (3 parts plastering sand, 1 part cement, ⅛ part fire clay or lime) for about 3 feet and screed it. Set the bricks in place firmly and butt them up to one another. After they have set, sweep in 30-mesh sand, just as for bricks on sand.

**Bricks in mortar:** It is more difficult to lay bricks in mortar than to lay them in sand. The value of the mortar joint (except where the ground freezes) is mostly aesthetic. In general, the mortar joint is not necessary for stability under normal mild weather conditions.

Dry mortar is relatively easy to work with, but will usually leave its mark on the brick. It is difficult to keep the mortar in the cracks, but the dry mortar method is a good process if you want a rustic, antiqued look to your paving.

Lay the bricks in sand as described above, but leave a ½-inch joint between them. Continue this until you have set all the bricks in place. The mixture to go between the bricks is made of 4 parts plastering sand and 1 part cement. Throw it out across the bricks and then sweep it into the cracks. Make sure the bricks are dry when you throw on the mortar mix or it will stick to them. Use a hand brush to push the mix between the bricks, then a broom to sweep away the excess. Once the mix is in place, wet the area with a fine spray, being careful not to splash any mortar out of the joints.

*SCREED SAND about 3 feet at a time. Once bricks are in place, screed next 3 feet, set bricks even with others.*

*WORK FORWARD from bricks already laid. Here the bricks are laid jack-on-jack and leveled with a mallet.*

*DRIVEWAY of bricks set with wide joints in dry mortar for worn look. A good method with broken bricks.*

*PARKING STRIP of bricks in wet mortar. Wire-cut bricks in running bond; "headers" are existing concrete.*

Let the mortar set for about 2 hours, then scrub each brick as clean as you can get it with a wet burlap sack. After the paving is completely dry, go over it with mortar cleaner.

Wet mortar is best if you want a clean, tooled, or shaped mortar joint between bricks. Bricks in wet mortar can be laid on any properly prepared base. Remember that if the base heaves or drops, repair work will be very difficult.

Brick paving in wet mortar is a difficult job for the home craftsman. The method used by professional bricklayers requires long practice. It is virtually impossible for the beginner to get a clean job using this method.

However, there is a technique that allows even the beginner to set bricks with wet mortar. It requires patience and takes time, but the product can be very handsome:

First wet the bricks, otherwise they will suck the water out of the mix and it won't hold. You can get them just wet enough by spraying them with a hose in the morning for an afternoon job.

Then lay them in a ½-inch mortar base leaving ½-inch joint between them, and let them set for about 4 hours. Then, with a flat, pointed trowel, push the mortar into the joints. (For this mortar, use 4 parts plastering sand, 1 part cement, no fire clay. Fire clay

helps make the mixture stick and this quality is not needed here.)

**Cleaning up** spilled mortar may be the first problem. Try to work as cleanly as possible; when you drop excess mortar on the bricks, you can save time and effort by wiping it up immediately with a wet piece of burlap.

To remove mortar that has dried on the bricks, use a solution of 9 parts of water to 1 part of muriatic acid.

First soak the area to be cleaned with a fine spray of water to saturate it and cut down the capillary action of the bricks. Let the water soak in. Brush the area with the acid solution (*caution:* Muriatic acid is dangerous, wear gloves and use a plastic bucket), and then rinse thoroughly with a hose to prevent acid burn stains from remaining on the bricks. It is a good idea to test-clean a brick before starting on a larger area. Be careful not to splash nearby plants that might be harmed by the acid.

Efflorescence—the white deposit that sometimes appears on brick paving after it is wetted by rain or hosing—is caused by water soluble salts in the bricks or in the setting bed rising to the surface through capillary action. When the water dries, the salts crystallize into a white crust. In most cases where common brick has been used, it will be a matter of years before the salts have all come to the surface and efflorescence ceases.

A stiff brush will remove the dried salts. Brush them loose and sweep them away. Don't try to hose them off, as the water will only drive them back down into the bricks and the process will begin all over again the next time the bricks are wet.

## Concrete

Most versatile of all garden paving materials is concrete. The surface can be plain and smooth enough for dancing or roller skating, or it can have a handcrafted, rough-textured look.

Because concrete is a plastic material, you can blend it with other materials and cast it into an endless number of shapes and forms. Circles, ovals, curves, and flowing lines can be handled more easily with concrete than with pre-formed materials. Where patterns of rectangles and squares are called for in a plan, concrete can be poured in forms to fit your specifications.

Concrete patios and walks may be topped with any one of many inviting colors. There are numerous earth tones from which to choose as well as black, green, yellow, umber, red, or any shades of these. You can do this yourself: Mix the color pigment with dry cement, combine with other materials as usual, and apply as the top layer of your concrete surface.

Concrete gives you more material for your money than any other hard paving surface.

The disadvantages of concrete can be considerable if it is handled thoughtlessly. A smooth, unrelieved slab will reflect heat and light into the house. Concrete is hard to the touch, cold in the winter, hot in the summer. Because it is porous, concrete shows stains.

**How to buy concrete:** It is possible to buy concrete for your own use in any one of the three following ways:

1. *Bulk dry materials.* You buy the required amounts of sand, cement, and gravel. Unless you have ample storage space, buy only what you will need for the project at hand. (You can also buy a sand-gravel mix to combine with the cement.)

Advantages: Buying the materials dry and in bulk is the cheapest way you can get them. You can mix any amount that is convenient for you to use.

Disadvantages: You must have a place where you can store sand and gravel. The sacks of cement must be kept absolutely dry. This generally means covered storage.

2. *Transit mix.* Concrete in this form is delivered to your door, ready to set in place.

Advantages: No mixing equipment is needed. It can be prepared according to any specifications before delivery. You get consistent, well mixed concrete. Cost for larger quantities is only slightly more than for bulk dry materials.

Disadvantages: An extra charge is made for delivery of any quantity under 2 cubic yards. Some plants will deliver as little as ½ cubic yard under this arrangement, but others will deliver nothing less than 1 yard. There is another extra charge for any time a truck must wait beyond a minimum interval while delivering materials. Delivery to the actual site is often difficult. The trucks are too large for some driveways.

3. *Dry ready-mix.* You can buy sacked dry mixtures containing correct proportions of sand, cement, and gravel for an all-purpose concrete suitable for most home uses. There are two sizes of sacks available—60 and 90 pounds.

Advantages: There is no guess work. All you have to do is add water, mix, and pour the concrete. It is ideal for patching old jobs or doing piecemeal work.

Disadvantages: It is quite expensive. The cost is about four times that of materials sold in the other two forms. Although it is a practical way for the

*GOURD-SHAPED PATIO of exposed aggregate repeats texture of dappled shade. Design: Nagoa Sakurai.*

home owner to buy concrete for a small job, it is usually not a good choice for very large jobs such as paving.

**Concrete finishes:** You have an unlimited range of textures when you do your own concrete finishing. Be sure that the finish you choose is the right one for the service it will perform:

1. *Smooth.* For the smoothest surface, use a steel trowel. Add a non-skid texture with a broom. Experiment with different bristled brooms to find out which of the many possible finishes you prefer. For the roughest "smooth" surface, use only the wood float—don't finish off with the steel trowel.

2. *Exposed aggregate.* One of the most popular patio surfaces, and one of the most difficult to handle, is exposed aggregate. Some contractors and craftsmen do the job with a hose, forcing out the top layer of mortar with the pressure from the spray. Others use a stiff wire brush or broom first, and then clean off excess mortar with the hose. It is difficult to make two jobs look alike, and many times different panels on a terrace or patio won't be consistently "exposed." However, the natural appearance won't ordinarily be spoiled by slight inconsistencies.

Make sure that your surface is level—a wood float finish is satisfactory. Then let concrete set up only until this top layer of mortar can be removed easily. Knowing when this stage has been reached takes at least a minimum of experience, or some experiment to get the "feel" of the material. If the concrete has set too firmly, it will be too late to remove the mortar. If the concrete is too wet, the exposed pebbles will come loose under the pressure of your hose or brush.

This job must be done in sections that can be worked at exactly the proper time. If you do let the concrete set too firmly, scrub the surface with a solution of muriatic acid and water. This will often remove some of the cement-and-sand mortar.

3. *Pebble mosaic.* Pebbles from the beach or a stream are pressed into a ½ or 1-inch layer of damp mortar laid over a 2 or 3-inch base of concrete. (If cars will drive over it, make the base 5 or 6 inches thick.) The mortar should be about 1 part cement to 2 parts of sand, with enough water for a mix that spreads easily but doesn't run. The mix should be elastic enough so that a little mortar moves up around each pebble.

The pebbles should be wet before being set into place. Check to see that they are keeping a true level surface by occasionally tapping with a long, straight board. You can add color to the mortar to match or complement the pebbles.

It is wise to lay out an approximate pattern on paper beforehand; but since you will have to work fast, some of the design will have to be freehand.

*STEPPING STONES 16 inches in diameter turn this garden into small patio; pebbles add pattern.*

*RELIEVE MONOTONY by altering finish—here a band of pebbled concrete. Design: Henry Y. Matsutani.*

PAVING, *rich green dichondra lawn complementary. Pebbled paving, smooth concrete squares alternated.*

ASPHALT *is inexpensive solution to large paved areas, but needs contrast of plants, brick or wood border.*

Since you are really working with an art form when you start a pebble mosaic, you can't estimate how much time it will take to do any particular job. You won't use more than one shovelful of mortar at any one time.

Choices in paving do not have to be as simple as either-or. You can drop a block of pebble mosaic in a brick area, or combine smooth stones with concrete, or play with contrasting colors and shapes, combining colored concrete, colored gravel, or brick.

By using larger stones, a cobbled effect can be achieved by pressing stones into a fairly stiff concrete mixture only to about half their thickness. This finish is not suitable for foot traffic. If you wish to have this type of finish for an area that will receive traffic, push the stones into the concrete and level. Different effects can be achieved by the use of stones of different size, color, and shape. Or you may vary one module from the next. Use your imagination.

## Asphalt

Asphalt offers a few unique advantages. It is a resilient material, with no glare. It gives back no heel clicks and absorbs rather than reflects sound. Asphalt is a good selection for paving for children's

play areas, driveways and utility areas. It provides a softer surface for spills from bikes and tricycles.

For best appearance, it needs the contrast of plants, brick, concrete, or wood borders.

For texture variation: After surface has been rolled once, scatter sand or pebbles, then roll again. With exposed colored pebbles in the surface, asphalt paving loses some of its parking lot look; with surface texture it seems more suitable in the garden.

It has a few disadvantages: If not given a solid foundation, it will sag and crack. Where summers are hot, it increases already hot temperatures. Its black surface causes it to absorb more heat than any other paving material. Heat softens it. The prints of sharp-toed furniture will show. It does not maintain a uniform color. Weeds and Bermuda grass will penetrate it.

The secret of good asphalt is a solid base of crushed rock, firmly compacted with a heavy roller. The base should be held in place by forms or headers so the edges of the asphalt won't crumble.

The hot-mixed, hot-applied asphaltic concrete is the most durable; it is the best to use if you have it contractor-applied with heavy equipment. One of the cold mixes is the choice for the gardener who is doing his own work. The handyman will need a heavy roller to compact the asphalt properly.

*HANDMADE CERAMIC TILE in* Sunset's *reception room, corridors, outdoor areas, gives finished look.*

*FLAGSTONE stepping stones accented by lacy look of pachysandra as ground cover. Path has natural look.*

### Tile

Tile is the most finished-looking of all the garden paving materials. It can be waxed for a gleaming, formal finish, good for dancing. This air of formality and the generous discipline of its pattern can overwhelm the small garden if it is not carefully used.

The most pleasing uses are on surfaces that are direct extensions of indoor areas, or under overheads where the house feeling rather than the garden feeling is uppermost.

The principal objection to tile is its high cost. The high quality materials and precision workmanship that go into its manufacture make tile much more costly than common brick.

There are several sizes, colors, and shapes to choose from. Outdoor floor tile is rough-surfaced in contrast to the glazed varieties used in kitchens and bathrooms. Patio tile comes in brick red; quarry tile is obtainable in tones running from gray to brick color. The large, foot-square tiles are commonly known as patio tile; the others—9 by 9, 6 by 6—are called quarry tile. Patio tile is not made to such close tolerances as quarry tile and consequently is cheaper per square foot.

To save cutting or chipping, plan out surface requirements to stay within the dimensions of the tile you intend to use. Allow ¾-inch mortar joints for the large tiles, ½-inch for small sizes.

For a permanent surface, set in a bed of sand mortar (5 parts of clean sand to 1 part cement). Push the mixture between tile; keep the area wet until all the mortar sets up. Tiles should be laid over a bed of concrete, as they are liable to become chipped or broken if put down over soil. They can also be laid on decking.

### Flagstone

Where the spirit of the garden is entirely natural, none of the man-made pavings seems appropriate. In situations such as a terrace on a wooded hillside where the paving is associated with ferns, flagstones come into their own.

Laid by a craftsman with the eye of an artist, flagstone can present the line and pattern and color of an abstract painting. The harder types give a surface as permanent as the house itself, and they will survive in cold where bricks fail. If you live in a severe-winter area, shop carefully, because soft flags are sold in many yards. Units should be scaled to the size of the area; in a heavily wooded area, play up the material's natural elemental qualities by using large scale blocks.

Care must be taken with flagstone to avoid a cold, quarry-like effect. The surface is sometimes rough or slippery.

Slabs can be irregular or roughly rectangular in shape. Thickness most often ranges from ½ to 2 inches, although sometimes you will get stones as thick as 6 inches. For paving over a sand bed, a 2-inch thickness is essential to prevent cracking; thinner stones are set over a concrete slab.

For limited areas such as walks, where soil is stable and well drained, flagstones can be put down directly over the soil. Dig out the soil to a depth slightly less than the thickness of the flags and fit them in place. Fill joints with turf, or pack in some good soil and plant grass seed, or set in clumps of a creeping ground cover.

For a permanent surface, set flagstones in a mortar bed on a 2-inch slab of concrete (1 part cement to 3 parts sand). Work in small areas—set only one or two flags at a time.

Whatever method you use, avoid getting a pattern that is too busy. Begin by laying all the stones loose, shifting them to please your eye.

## Adobe blocks

Adobe is a traditional material in California and Arizona. Informal and an ideal earth color for garden paving, it is an exceptionally flattering background for flower colors. It is soft looking, without glare or reflection.

The usual block is 8 inches wide, 16 inches long, and 4 inches thick. Such a unit weighs 30 pounds. Two sizes of adobe blocks are also available which weigh less and can be used as a veneer—4 x 16 x 4, 12 x 16 x 4. Because dimensions vary slightly, adobe blocks are usually difficult to lay in patterns that call for snug fittings. Open joints, ¾ to 1 inch, compensate for irregularities.

Like brick, adobe blocks can be laid on a sand bed. Take care that the bed is solid, stable, and quite level—the blocks will not bridge a hollow or straddle a hump without cracking when weight is put upon them. Joints may be filled with dirt, sand, or dry mortar. A dirt filling permits crevice planting.

Buy extra blocks for replacements—a few may develop flaws or disintegrate. It is difficult to match the color and texture later.

Unless there is an adobe maker in your locality, transportation costs will rule out this material.

*ADOBE BLOCKS in* Sunset's *patio are used in combination with hand-finished tile. Blocks are an inch apart on a sand base; the interspaces are filled with soil for plantings. Blocks look like swept earth.*

## Crushed rock and gravel

Paths of crushed rock or gravel do not call attention to themselves and they feel as natural underfoot as a mountain trail. In service and storage areas, this material is as practical as it is inexpensive.

There are disadvantages. Weeds will grow in the gravel if not controlled. There are two ways of doing this: One is to use weed killers. The other method that has proven successful for long-term control of weeds is to place plastic sheeting such as 4 mil polyethylene beneath the gravel. Be sure to perforate it in a few places to allow rain to drain away; then cover with 2 inches or more of gravel. The rocks also will spread into plant beds and lawns, but this problem can be lessened by confining the path or area with header boards.

You can buy crushed or uncrushed gravel. Crushed gravel is man-made from larger rocks. The uncrushed kind is natural gravel, rounded by the action of glaciers, streams, and the sea.

In the grading process, gravel is washed over screens with apertures of various sizes. Gravel is commonly available in the following sizes (diameter in inches): ¼, ½, ¾, and 1½.

A standard size for patio floors is ½-inch crushed. Smallest size obtainable is called pea gravel, a rounded, river-washed (uncrushed) type.

Rounded, uncrushed gravel is often used for the exposed aggregate finish. Laid loose, it is not satisfactory — the stones roll underfoot. Crushed gravel packs better, and when rolled makes a fairly firm surface. Gravel stands up best when put down over a more permanent bed of base rock or decomposed granite. But it will give several seasons' service when put right on the ground.

**The usual method of application** is to spread a 2-inch layer, rake, dampen, and roll with a heavy roller or hand tamp. Most contractors recommend ½-inch rock; however, some landscape architects say you can use any size you like—as long as you put down a layer only the thickness of one piece of gravel. Roll into soil or any other binding agent; renew, rake, and re-roll as necessary.

## Base rocks, decomposed granite, sandy gravel, redrock

These and other similar names, differing by localities, designate a general class of fill material—part rock and part dirt—taken from hillsides and often used as a base for asphalt paving. They can also be used to surface garden paths and secondary areas. Ideally, the "fines" and larger aggregate compact to form a water-repellent, non-dusting surface. Too much dirt among the rocks makes the surface impassable when wet. Too much rock in relation to dirt makes it stay loose and crumbly.

A good way to handle these materials is to put them down in three or more 1-inch layers; dampen, and then roll or hand tamp.

Advantages: These materials are comparatively inexpensive and quickly applied, easy to maintain, and can be used as a base for later paving.

Disadvantages: Some kinds get muddy in rainy weather. They track into the house.

## Red lava rock

Red lava rock gives an excellent color contrast to plants; however, it is too intense a color for large areas. It is not especially durable, and may track; it turns to powder under traffic. It is best used as an accent in small areas that receive light traffic.

## Roof rock

In areas where paving gets very little traffic and in pattern paving, the green, tan, or white roof rock is useful for color.

## Wood rounds

Wood rounds used as a paving material contribute warm color and soft texture to the garden. One or two placed in a flower bed give you a place to step when you weed or water; several of them set almost flush with the ground make an unobtrusive walk through the garden, or you can pave an entire patio or terrace with them.

Wooden rounds have the advantage of being in good supply, though not always easy to find. They are usually less expensive than brick or concrete, and require no special skills to set in place.

Count as a disadvantage wood's limited life, as compared with concrete or stone. Wood becomes slippery when wet, and if used in the shade, may acquire a treacherous skin of moss. Rough sawn wooden rounds provide good traction. Sharp sand spread on the surface also helps. Three factors influence the length of time wood will last in the ground: the kind of wood you use, the ground you set it in, and whether or not you treat it. Wood decays most quickly in poorly drained, heavy, or very rich soil. Rounds last longest when set on a 1 to 3-inch-thick base of sand or gravel. Where summers are warm and dry, wood may warp.

Treating with a preservative will add years to the life of your wood rounds. To inhibit decay, paint (out of doors) with a preservative compound containing pentachlorophenol, brushing well into all

*RANDOM-SIZED ROUNDS of maple and fir set into the slope function as steps between patio and terrace.*

*BETWEEN rock wall and sidewalk, uncrushed gravel looks neat, adds decorative touch, discourages weeds.*

surfaces twice, allowing the wood to dry for two weeks between applications, longer in cold or wet weather. Chemicals may be toxic to adjacent plants, so rinse rounds with water and let dry for a day before setting in the ground.

Lumber companies and some nursery and garden centers carry rounds or can get them for you. A few plywood mills saw butt ends of logs unsuitable for plywood into rounds. Small outlying lumber mills, particularly those that split cedar shakes, will often cut cedar rounds to order.

Though four inches is the standard thickness of a round, many landscape architects specify rounds six to eight inches thick. The added thickness gives them more stability underfoot. When blocks begin to decay in the center, dig out punky wood and fill with concrete. For rough, non-slip treads, lay in pebbles before concrete sets.

## Bark

Next to the pine needle floor beneath old forests, bark is the most natural surface in color and walking "feel" offered to the gardener. It has a good, reddish color, is soft and springy, and is not harmed by moisture. Since it scatters easily, it is best confined between header boards. Use it on a path, as a generous cushion for a play yard, or in a part of the garden leading out to a natural, woodsy area. It is used in municipal and school playgrounds under equipment that is used actively by the children—swings, jungle gyms, slides, rings, etc.

Put right on top of the soil for a path, but over 2 or 3 inches of gravel (for drainage) in a play yard. When the bark wears out, it still makes excellent compost. Buy the bark that is the most readily available in your area—redwood, fir, pine—any kind of bark will give good service.

### Tricks of the trade

By leaving generous open spaces for planting, you can make any paving material cover a much larger area and achieve the feeling of a bigger patio.

You can use 180 square feet of paving in this manner:

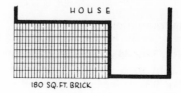

Or, by adding 10 square feet of brick and two areas of planting, you can double the size of your patio:

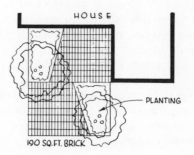

Or, you can make the space apparently larger by freeing it from the house and tying it to a unit of planting:

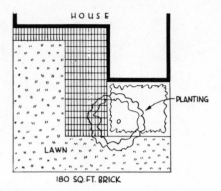

180 SQ. FT. BRICK

Or, you can enlarge the patio and still keep the feeling of brick by combining it with a cheaper material such as concrete:

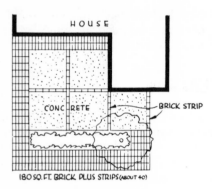

180 SQ. FT. BRICK PLUS STRIPS (ABOUT 40)

### Tips on handling concrete

Concrete is heavy. Make it and mix it close to where you will want to use it. If your yard slopes, remember that it is easier to let a loaded wheelbarrow roll downhill than to push it uphill.

Any foreign matter tends to weaken the concrete. Water should be clean and, most important of all, sand and gravel should be free of dirt or vegetation.

Concrete will set up more quickly on a hot, dry day than on a cool, damp one. Never mix more than you will be able to use in an hour's time.

Wood eventually will rot in concrete. To retard this action, you can treat header boards with pentachorophenol or creosote.

Never attempt to re-mix concrete that has begun to set.

Unfortunately, most ready-mix plants don't operate on Saturday or Sunday. Be sure to check with the ones in your area before you make any plans for week-end concrete projects.

For measuring ingredients: When you hand-mix concrete on a flat surface, the bottomless box sketched below is a welcome time-saver for measuring dry materials. The 6-inch boards are your measuring lines. Full, the box holds 2 cubic feet. After measuring, lift the box off and you are ready to start the mixing.

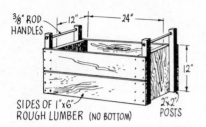

For checking the slope: So that it will drain properly, you will want some slope on any large area of paving. A drop of 1 inch per 6 feet is usually quite adequate.

### Header boards

From a practical standpoint, it is impossible to consider paving—concrete, asphalt, gravel, or brick—without considering header boards.

Header boards have established their place in the home garden. They make a neat demarcation between lawns and plants, they keep grass and weeds out of plant beds, and they hold water within the root area of shrubs and plants. They also make handsome edging and division strips in brick, concrete, or other garden paving.

Redwood and cedar are the woods most often used, since they contain their own preservative. You can leave them alone, or treat them with any of the commercial preservatives; the difference in longevity won't be considerable.

**Here are some rules** to follow when installing wood edging:

To prevent the lumber from splitting (particularly the stakes), use galvanized box nails (similar to common nails, but thinner). Blunting the points of the nails also helps. And place a back-up block—sledge, crowbar, rock, or block of wood—against the opposite side of the edging when driving the nails.

The most popular edgings are made of 2 by 4-inch lumber, either rough cut (2 inches thick), or finished lumber (1½ inch thick). The 1½-inch thickness is about the minimum for a sturdy edging, but is usually quite ample. (You can use 3 by 4 or 4 by 4 lumber for heavier edgings, if all the headers are to be in straight lines.)

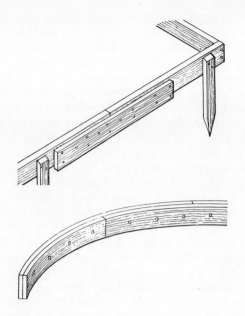

*HEADER BOARDS. Splices can be 1 by 4's or 2 by 4's, 2 feet long. For curves, laminate 2 or more boards.*

To form a curved edging, you nail the thinner, more flexible boards together until the laminated board is the thickness desired around the curve. Many lumber yards carry "resawn" board (½ and 1 inch thick) in stock for curved edgings. The ½-inch resawn boards are usually far from uniform—they vary from 5/16 to 5/8 inch in thickness. The trick here is to measure the approximate radius of the curve you wish to form, then go to the lumberyard and try bending different "½-inch" thicknesses to find which will make the curve. Choose the thickest boards that will do, because thin ones tend to rot and splinter more readily. You can soak the thicker boards with water on the job, if necessary, to make the bending easier.

Dig shallow trenches in which to place the boards, with their top edges either flush with the ground or slightly above. Use 1 by 2 or wider stakes (you can buy pointed stakes at many lumberyards). Place a stake at least every 5 feet, also one close to each corner, and place one on each side of a splice.

If your edging simply divides two cultivated areas, you can alternate the stakes on opposite sides of the edging. If it borders a lawn, place all stakes and splices away from the grass so that you will be able to run a lawn edger along the edging without any interference.

If possible, drive stakes with a 4-pound sledge or heavy hammer because repeated blows with a lightweight hammer do more damage to the ends of the stakes. You can drive the stakes an inch below the top of the edging or, for the neatest job, cut them off at a slant. To drive a stake below the top without damaging it, first hammer it level with the edging, then hammer on another stake held crosswise over it. Place two or more nails in each stake. Place any necessary splice an inch below the top of the edging, and use at least eight nails at each splice.

On curves, stake one of the thinner pieces in place, then nail the succeeding pieces to it. Be generous with nails, and stagger joints. When you are done, drive some extra-long nails completely through the built-up edging (particularly at any point where the laminations tend to separate), bend the nails over, and clinch them.

**For easier stake driving:** One way to make the job of driving stakes easier is to use steel tent stakes (available at most sporting goods stores). These stakes, made of bent sheet steel, have two edges that bite into the side of the header board and hold it very securely.

These are other ways to make wooden stakes go into the ground more easily:

1. Use a sharply pointed round stake (an old broom handle is long enough for two or three stakes) to make a preliminary hole. This hole will serve as opening for a larger square stake (about 2 inches thick).

2. Let a trickle of water run down into the hole into which you are driving the stake. Water will soften the soil below the point of the stake.

## GARDEN SCREENS

Once you think of a garden as space to live in, you have a whole new set of requirements for its planning. You think of it more as a room than as a piece of ground. And you expect and desire much the same visual privacy you would enjoy in an indoor living room.

No matter how friendly you are with your neighbors, you have no right to embarrass them by making them watch your outdoor activities. For outdoor dining, entertaining, sun-bathing, or just sitting and talking with a friend, you need at least a semblance of privacy. Privacy means walls or screens of some kind. In an outdoor room, the walls may be of trees, shrubs, vines, brick, stone, wood, and other materials. The walls and screens may or may not be on the perimeter of the lot. You may consider the garden room as a room within the garden.

In several localities, fences along highways, arterials, or railroads must be either chain-link wire or masonry. The concrete block fence is a basic fence in many Southern California localities. Several subdividers provide a 4-foot concrete block wall with the house. Since the 4-foot height is not enough for privacy, new home owners face the problem of increasing the height. One way is to drive pipe or iron into the wall and string wire for vines. Another way

of increasing height of concrete fence to bring necessary privacy is to attach panels of grapestakes, lattice, or other light wood to the face of the wall. Such panels can be made as screens or left open and planted with vines.

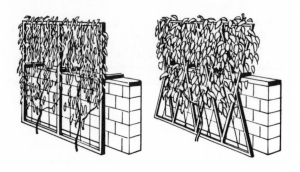

The amateur builder finds concrete blocks easy to handle for low fences and walls. All walls should be built up on a level, continuous foundation of concrete wider than the wall. The concrete block can be set up dry—without mortar. The final step of pouring concrete into the cells of the blocks can be taken when you feel like doing it.

If you object to the machine-made appearance of the concrete, you can lay up the blocks with mortar. If the joints are not raked and the wall is painted, the mechanical look is lost.

In choosing materials for walls, it's well to remember that your selection need not be just the choice between building material or plant material. It can be a pleasant combination of both. A hedge along property lines seems less offensive than a fence to some people, but a completely surrounding hedge may seem just as confining as a fence. Shrubs, trees and fences can be combined and each element can benefit from the presence of the other.

Where space permits, you can enclose with masses of foliage. Such enclosures are not to be had immediately. A home owner on an interior lot in a new subdivision is joined by five neighbors (counting the two at the rear corners). More and more often nowadays, his living room and all the neighbors' living rooms open into the back garden. How can he use his garden?

He doesn't want to wait three years for shrubs and trees to give him privacy. The obvious answer is a fence. The need for fences is so universal in such cases that many newly built subdivisions in the West provide the fence with the house. The usual method is to enclose the back garden completely with a 6-foot board fence on the property line.

Left to itself, the 6-foot board fence creates a rigid, confining, boarded-up feeling. It isn't too high for the eye, but it pens you in, and you sense other pens around you. Nothing is gained by lowering the height of the fence. Anything less than 6 feet is useless as a privacy screen. Even a 6-foot fence does not block out the view of neighbors' heads and shoulders if houses are even a foot above ground level.

Planning the walls of your garden room calls for an entirely different set of judgments from planning the walls of an indoor room. Six feet indoors is entirely different from 6 feet outdoors. In an indoor room, the lines of sight are almost constantly below the 6-foot level. Walking through the house you watch the floor far more than either ceiling or walls. In conversation, the lines of sight are seldom above the 4-foot level.

In an outdoor room, the eye is more conscious of the tall trees and sky than of the floor of the garden. Even a 6-foot fence is just a part of the wall of the garden room. The house roofs next door, the trees a block away, the hills beyond, the clouds in the sky, all combine to make the wall and ceiling of your garden. Your problem is to work with all of the elements to create a pleasing environment, of which the fence is only one part.

The nature of a fence can be changed by vines, or low shrubs. Trees can be used to screen out what you don't want to see and can also frame views that are pleasant.

Even though the fence is just a part of the garden enclosure, it is prominent enough to cause those who design suburban gardens to focus a great deal of attention on its design. In the past just about every possible variation in design has been tried.

After trying everything, the commercial fence builder has found that the most acceptable fence is a simple one, built with 4 by 4 posts, 8 feet apart, with 2 by 4 stringers. The popular commercial fences include a basket-weave design using ½-inch boards horizontally, and straight line arrangements using 1-inch boards horizontally or vertically. Of these, the fence with vertical boards is usually the most unobtrusive. In a subdivision, you get either the outside or inside of this fence.

One argument in favor of this fence is that it can be changed without much trouble. By working with your neighbor, you can easily change the fence to alternating panels, or you can lessen the confining

*TALL, WIDE HEDGE around property; few trees adapt better than Western hemlock (Tsuga heterophylla).*

*COMBINATION of fence, Thuja pyramidalis hedge. Green plants soften the starkness of fence alone.*

quality of a perimeter fence by giving it a see-through panel or two. The boundaries of the lot are less distinct. If wire or a plastic-covered wire panel is backed by interesting plant material, the effect of more space is even more pronounced. In changing from boards to a light material, use an additional stringer and brace.

If you do not wish to knock out boards or alter the existing fence, the addition of light members—such as 1 by 1's and 1 by 2's—will relieve the heaviness of the fence. If the light members are painted a contrasting color, the slender vertical lines will dominate. If the fence is treated as a series of panels, you'll find yourself working out panel design and using similar panel units in other parts of the garden. In a deep lot, there is much to be gained by using a screen fence to set aside a section for a cut flower garden, storage, compost, or other garden requirements.

The use of screens within the property line, with or without perimeter fencing, permits many interesting divisions of space—rooms within the garden room. In dividing the garden into smaller areas, take care that space flows between all areas of the garden. It is possible to make the total appear to be larger by dividing it.

Don't forget as you work with the fence that it can be changed more by planting than by construction. One of the best ways to make the boundaries of your garden less distinct is to plant so that por-tions of the fence disappear. Some of the most important materials used for enclosing a garden room are the tall shrubs that don't take up much space. See pages 145-159.

Generally in localities where ordinances limit the perimeter fence to 6 feet in height, the height of structures inside the setback lines is not limited. For example, a wall of the house or garage can be carried out at eave level; a vine trellis can be 8 feet or more when inside the setback lines. Watch for these opportunities when looking for ways to screen winds or views that are not controllable by the 6-foot fence.

The use of materials other than wood in portions of the fence is most practical when the fence is constructed in a series of panels. This is especially true when you plan with the idea that fence sections can easily be used as independent panels, screens, or baffles.

For special panels in the fence, consider any and all building materials that will stand the weather—asbestos, aluminum, plastic, glass, plywood, reed screen, composition board, and wire.

Generally panel materials are more easily and less wastefully assembled if used in modules equal to the standard size of the material. Plywood, asbestos, and other sheet materials are commonly available in panels 4 by 8 feet. This size sheet works smoothly into an 8-foot section of a 6-foot fence. With one knife or sawcut, the material can be sized to fit.

Certain materials have characteristics and qualities that make them more adaptable for certain uses:

1. *Asbestos-cement* panels are a heavy, compact material that stops both vision and motion. They "resist" children—they are almost harmproof. They are indestructible in sun, rain, cold. These panels are especially suitable for use in children's play yards as a baffle, wind screen, and even as a blackboard. (Chalk writing washes off easily with water.)

2. *Fiberglass* is a translucent material that can be obtained in various permanent colors—in flat or corrugated form. When applied to a frame correctly, it will not break or scuff easily. It is especially useful in dark areas where a solid frame would cut off light. Be certain to buy good quality material to insure a fence with a long life. Consult your building material dealer.

3. *Glass* can solve the problem when the best view is located in the same direction as hard-blowing, cold, prevailing wind. It is valuable in interior lots where wind protection is necessary within a garden. To avoid breakage, the usual solution is to make the wall part wood and part glass.

4. *Plywood* can be used in any part of the garden. Its smooth finish is usually stained or painted to withstand the weather. It is frequently used as an element of simplicity to contrast with some more exciting form, color, texture or shadow. If you buy plywood for garden use, remember to specify "exterior grade."

5. *Plastic-coated screen* is translucent and light in feeling, and it blurs out anything located behind it. These qualities make it excellent for use in dark corners where privacy is preferred, and in a small side yard, or cramped area. Because you can actually see forms and shadows on the other side of the screen, you get an effect of spaciousness rather than of enclosure.

6. *Wire* comes in many mesh sizes and gauges. It is frequently used in conjunction with a pool area; when the pool is not in use, the wire fence keeps out people but doesn't block the view or breeze. A heavy wire fence solves many play yard problems—parents can see in and children can see out.

7. *Vines,* grown over a wire framework, can be functional as well as decorative. A warm breeze that passes through a moist vine fence into the garden usually aids in cooling the garden.

8. *Aluminum panels* are available in many colors and sizes. These panels will provide complete protection and are very durable.

## The screen enclosure

If you enclose an area with screen—the old fly screen or one of its modern counterparts—you accomplish three things: wind control, insect control, and sun control. A square foot of most metal screening covers as much as 25 to 30 per cent of that area with metal. This metal barrier in turn cuts about 30 per cent of the sun's intensity and slows a breeze to a standstill.

When screen is used in both walls and roof, the enclosed area becomes a quiet, airy, protected place for people and plants. A screen roof will collect

*TRANSLUCENT PLASTIC panels can be used to set off plants—look what they do for nandina.*

*FREE-STANDING SCREEN angled to block only portion of view which prevented terrace from being private.*

leaves and twigs and will need an occasional sweeping to keep it looking neat. Unless you are a stickler for neatness, however, the dappled shade pattern made by sunlight filtering through the leaves can be rather pleasant.

In designing the screened-in area, remember that the more lofty the overhead and the more generous the floor space, the more luxurious will be the enclosure. There is a world of difference between this kind of enclosure and the old, screened porch.

Many homes lend themselves to screened rooms. There are several ways to screen in a patio or terrace. The easiest, most economical method is to use roll screening. By applying the screening directly to the structure, you avoid the additional expense of separate frames for each opening. Tack or staple the screens on to stay if they must be left on in winter weather.

Instead of bulk roll screening, you can use tension or roller-type screens. Both types are more expensive than roll screening, but can be protected from winter weather. (Roller screens roll up out of sight, tension screens can be removed quickly.) Roller screens usually require professional installation. Or you can build your own frames out of 1 by 2-inch stock, a suitable molding, and cut roll screening.

## GARDEN SHELTER

Overhead structures increase the amount of comfortable living space for people, and they also provide protected growing space for plants. To many gardeners, the most beautiful and useful overhead is a tree. Depending upon the kind of tree you select, you have your choice of deep or filtered shade, high or low shade, all-year shade or summer shade and winter sun. One wide-spreading tree can eventually shade a 60-foot garden. Six small trees will give you shade more quickly, and do it without dominating the garden.

For home owners with a sun problem that needs a solution right now, trees are too slow. An overhead for immediate sun control is the lath structure. You can control with exactness the amount of sun you or your plants will receive by the size and placement of the lath.

Another type of overhead structure is the vine support. This generally is a light structure that gives some protection while the vine is taking over. The lightly framed overhead offers the designer many opportunities for quick effects.

Still another type of structure aimed at sun control is the overhead holding more or less perishable materials, such as reed, bamboo, netting, or canvas. Most of these are low in cost and, even when replaced every five years, are not too expensive.

*SUNSHADE under which plants can thrive. Upper shade, 12 feet high at point, rises to 15 feet over eave.*

Overheads that directly extend indoor space and are attached to the house are in another class. The open-air, all-weather rooms that they create usually should be designed and constructed with an eye to their future incorporation into the house itself. As a potential room of the house, this type of overhead should have an architectural similarity and continuity with the house.

You may decide to combine several types of roof enclosure in one structure. You may want a combination that will give you livable space in the rainy season, in the heat of summer, and in the cool, breezy season. Or you may vary your materials simply to achieve a pleasant effect.

Here's how the various types of materials have been used, how they are built, and how they fit into the garden plan.

### Lath

The term lath is used to cover a variety of materials. Common ⅜ by 1-inch lath will sag and twist if not supported every 24 inches. Small dimension lumber —1 by 1's or, preferably, 1 by 2's and 1 by 3's—is more satisfactory. The most commonly used lumber is ⅜ x 1½ redwood.

The use of lath has changed dramatically in the last few years. Many years ago a lathhouse was a small structure built to protect plants. Today we make a distinction between the lathhouse (a plant shelter) and a lath overhead. The lofty overhead does not take up garden space as does the small lathhouse for plants alone.

*OVERHEAD COVERED with reed screening runs along side of house and extends to shade plants, house.*

*ENGAWA roofed to provide summer shade for people and plants, but to catch the warm winter sun.*

### Woven reeds and bamboo blinds

These materials provide more densely filtered shade than the lath roof; they are preferred over wood lath by many home owners because the shade pattern is more natural and has less contrast. Both are effective wind screens. Neither is considered a permanent material. We have seen 5-year-old installations in California that were still presentable.

Reed and bamboo are good materials for partially enclosing a high lath-covered frame. By various combinations of lath overhead and reed or bamboo, you can direct shade where you want it. The western sun can be partially or completely blocked depending upon how low you drop the reed on the west side. In some cases, adjustable protection is welcome on all sides of the overhead.

### Canvas

The virtue of canvas is its versatility. It can be held in place overhead with wires, pipe frame, or wood. If held on wires, it can be extended or folded back as the weather requires. When used as an overhead in hot summer areas, take care that a warm-air trap is not created beneath it. Many new fixtures for the construction of canvas shelters have been manufactured in recent years. In addition, canvas is available in all colors of the rainbow—in solid colors, stripes, checks or plaids.

In the West where summer rains are no problem, there are some advantages in keeping overhead shelters two or three feet out from the house. Open space prevents the house from being darkened and allows full growth of plants along the house.

One of the smartest canvas installations consists of panels of canvas, fitted with grommets and laced to a pipe frame. In most cities you'll find awning companies that specialize in the use of canvas in the garden. From them you can get anything from complete installation down to prefabricated units of pipe frame or panels with grommets.

### Fiberglass

Panels of fiberglass solve several types of overhead problems. Because they form a rainproof roof without cutting out light, they are valuable in overheads in cool-summer areas where sunlight is never intense. In hot-summer areas, this material is used on the east side of the house. Don't use it, especially in light colors, as a sun filter where summers are hot.

Fiberglass panels are often used in combination with opaque corrugated materials, such as asbestos board, and with aluminum panels. Because they admit light, they are useful in situations where a solid roof would darken the inside rooms of a house.

The quality of fiberglass has been much improved, extending the life and usefulness of the material. Many new colors are available in a variety of textures. Buy good quality for long life and good looks.

## Corrugated aluminum and asbestos

This material gives complete overhead protection. Aluminum is noisy in the wind if not carefully installed, and will expand and contract with heat and cold, loosening ordinary fastenings. Unless properly nailed on, it will leak around the nail holes. Check with your building materials supplier on the latest type of fasteners. Many colors are available in aluminum panels; choose one to suit your situation.

## Louvered window screen

The use of this material demands a careful study of sun angles before installation; the degree of shade depends upon the direction of the louvers and the time of day. It solves the problem of screening the wind without blocking ventilation; however, it gives no rain protection and, because leaves and small particles lodge in the tiny louvers, it can become untidy under trees.

Miniature louvers are built right into this screening material. It is made in a variety of finishes, the most commonly available and economical being aluminum. It is long-lasting and requires very little maintenance.

## Ordinary fly screen

This is valuable where insects bother or where you need wind controls. A screened enclosure 10 to 12 feet high gets away from any feeling of being caged in, and creates a quiet, protected environment for people and for plants. This material is also available with a plastic coating.

## LIGHTING

Garden lighting should be considered from three points of view:

1. To illuminate paths, walks, steps, and living areas for use at night.

2. To illuminate and dramatize plant material.

3. To use light as a substitute for plants—in other words, to garden with light.

To the home owner with undeveloped plant material, night lighting is sheer magic. With a few well placed lights, he can create a picture as romantic as Rio or Hawaii. A light panel in a fence, a shaded light on a post shining down on a pot of white petunias, the reflected light from canvas—these can transform an everyday little garden into another more dramatic world.

Whether your garden is new and sparse or old and rich with plant material, the light you design with will be of these kinds:

*Direct light.* Light goes from source directly to the tree, vine, flower, pool, or whatever object is to be lighted. The direct source—the globe—in all cases should be hidden.

*Indirect light.* The light goes from the source to a reflecting surface which directs it to the area or object to be lighted. Direct the light to the ceiling of an outdoor room and let it reflect down, rather than directing the light from the ceiling.

*Glow light.* The light itself becomes the object to be seen and adds very little illumination. Light is covered with translucent material such as frosted glass, plastic, paper, or parchment.

Permanent outdoor lights must be weatherproof. There are a number of standard units available. Using the basic waterproof socket and connection,

*PROTECTED PATIO on south side of house, with glass roof, offers ideal conditions for subtropicals.*

*ONE SMALL low voltage fixture throws guiding light above, on doors, walk below. Warm, welcome light.*

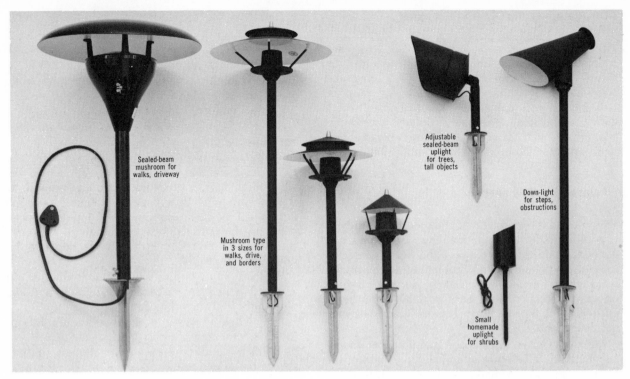

*HERE IS A SELECTION of low voltage garden fixtures that are available. Most can be purchased from electrical suppliers, hardware stores, and nurseries. All shown are waterproof, and all use 12-volt current.*

you can assemble many very effective types of light. A piece of tin 10 inches square can be bent and fixed to the side of a post or a fence to give a soft light. Wood pieces, 1 by 6 or 1 by 8, are used in the same manner as tin. Large panels of light—using color—work well on a fence or wall.

Arranging for night lighting is best done by trial. The important thing is to avoid harsh light, to baffle the source of light. You can see what night lighting will do for you very inexpensively with temporary lighting. Here are points to check in making a permanent outdoor lighting installation.

Underground wiring, limited for years to lead-sheathed wire or cable in watertight rigid conduit, is now available in a chemically coated variety that can be buried directly in the ground. No conduit is necessary. The nonmetallic trench cable is obtainable as single-wire, two-wire, and three-wire conductors. If outlets are to be provided for outdoor appliances—such as electric hedge clippers, lawn mowers and trimmers, barbecue accessories—the outlet should be grounded to minimize shock hazard. Outlet boxes attached to a conduit system are self-grounded, but those used with trench cable usually need to be grounded with bare copper wire. Three-hole outlets are recommended with grounded, outdoor installations. Many electric tools marketed for garden use are now sold with 3-wire cords and 3-pronged plugs. Grounding of outdoor lighting circuits is a good practice, but not essential.

Trench for cables should be dug before walks and lawns are in. It's a good idea to carry out an extra cable for future extension. Bury cable at least 18 inches underground to avoid injuring it when spading the ground. Or, if shallower, protect the cable with a 1 by 3 or 1 by 4 board. Like this:

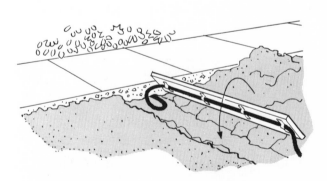

This cable must be given mechanical protection where it enters and leaves the ground. This can be done with conduit, pipe, or redwood frame, as illustrated on the next page.

Terminate cable in weatherproof outlet boxes with spring shut gasket covers or screw cap covers. Generally, the weatherproof convenience outlets should be placed near the ground in several locations so that inexpensive portable lights can be used.

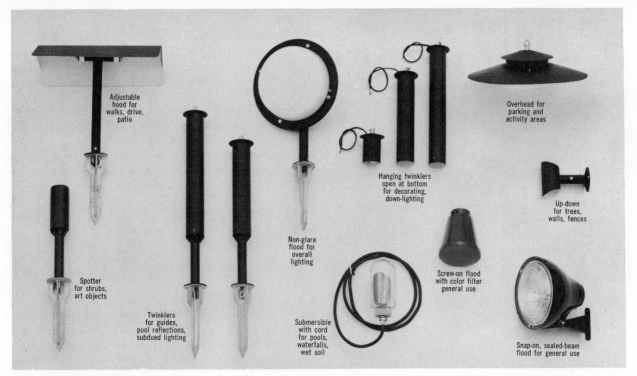

Adjustable
hood for
walks, drive,
patio

Overhead for
parking and
activity areas

Hanging twinklers
open at bottom
for decorating,
down-lighting

Up-down
for trees,
walls, fences

Non-glare
flood for
overall
lighting

Spotter
for shrubs,
art objects

Screw-on flood
with color filter
general use

Twinklers
for guides,
pool reflections,
subdued lighting

Submersible
with cord
for pools,
waterfalls,
wet soil

Snap-on, sealed-beam
flood for general use

*THERE ARE low voltage fixtures for all purposes. Lights for steps, mushroom types for drives, floods for overall lighting, twinklers for decorating, overheads for parking and activity areas, spotters for plant accents.*

Switches may be mounted inside the house or garage. Weatherproof switches and combination outlets and switches are available. If outdoor type is used, inset in fence posts or wall.

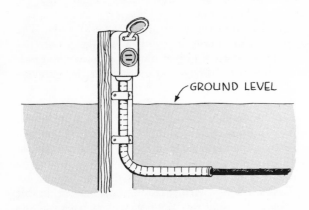

GROUND LEVEL

Don't overload any household circuit. An average 15-amp circuit can safely handle only about 1,500 watts. This would mean a maximum of 10 of the 150 watt flood light if no load is drawn off in the house. For normal lighting, No. 14 wire is large enough. When appliances are added, use No. 12. Check local building codes. Be certain to get a permit from the electrical inspector.

## Low-voltage lighting

Often heralded as a new development is low-voltage (l-v) lighting. It is really not new—for decades we have had it for our automobiles—but its use in our gardens is relatively new in concept and, with today's equipment, it can bring exciting advantages.

One of the most important is safety. A child can remove the bulb from any 12-volt garden light fixture and poke his fingers inside without a chance of receiving a dangerous electrical shock. If you inadvertently cut a 12-volt cable with a shovel or cultivator, there may be a spark, but no shock. You can even go to the extreme of making connections under-water, without feeling a tingle.

Another important advantage is the ease of installation. For l-v lighting, you need a transformer to reduce your 120-volt household current to the 12-volt current required. Most modern garden-light transformers simply plug into any handy outlet. From the transformer on, the 12-volt wiring is simply buried a few inches in the ground, strung along fences, and run up tree trunks—without the need of conduit or protected cable, as would be necessary with 120-volt wiring.

You can install it yourself, without experience or qualms. If you do not have the time, an electrician can install it throughout your garden at much less cost than 120-volt wiring. And you can easily adjust or move the l-v light fixtures years from now as your needs change and your plants grow.

The ease of installing l-v garden lighting also allows you to have what we call low-key lighting. You may have noticed a version of this in some restaurants—small hidden lights giving subdued, glareless illumination, often with a few other small hidden spotlights to dramatize features and give depth to the room. An even better example is the spectacle of a full moon rising over a clear high-altitude horizon to bathe a mountain scene with sparkling and glareless light, and bring distinct shadows and silhouettes to the landscape.

Such low-key lighting is not only ample for illumination but extremely flattering to your garden, patio, and entryways. It lets you create shadows and silhouettes with plants, lets you accent architectural features—quite the opposite of the common device of placing floodlights under the house eaves. With such floodlighting the entry or garden, as seen from the house, is strongly illuminated for a short distance away, but the light is flat and monotonous. You can see when you walk outdoors but not so well when you turn around, because of the glare.

Creating the delightful low-key effect is a matter of experimenting with light in different places and different ways in your garden. With l-v equipment, you or your electrical contractor can simply string the wiring on top of the ground, and leave it there for weeks, if necessary, until you decide exactly where each fixture should be placed.

Be sure to experiment at night. At least one large manufacturer of l-v fixtures today demands that contractors using his equipment locate all garden lights at night—it is the only way to be sure of the effect. Try a light under a shrub, over it, behind it. Try one in a garden pool, and also alongside it, reflecting on the water. The difference can be surprising, as can the difference made by moving a light just a few inches.

Every garden is different, but here are some factors that lighting experts keep in mind on almost all l-v installations:

Tend to use six or more small lights throughout your garden, rather than using two or three more powerful lights.

Place lights out beyond your patio. There, they create depth in the garden, and they draw insects away from the patio.

Install separate switches for bright "activity" lights, such as near a barbecue or table tennis area, so they can be turned off when not needed.

Consider using a few small lights on a fence or hedge, if needed, as a curtain between your garden and a neighbor's.

Be cautious in the use of color filters. A colored light can be handsome in a garden pool or waterfall, but it can destroy the nighttime beauty of flowers and plants.

Light the hazards as well as the attractive features. You know where a garden step is, but guests may not. Use submersible fixtures in wet areas and garden pools, or else waterproof the connections thoroughly with a rubber seam compound. You can place any l-v fixture in water, but exposed connections will corrode and fail in time.

Try placing a large mushroom light near the street end of your entryway, and smaller mushroom lights near the house. This gives an impression of depth and distance.

Overall, try to feature the effects of your garden lighting, rather than the source.

**Installing a l-v transformer**

It is best to choose a transformer of about 100-watt capacity for your garden and patio—so you can run 6 to 10 lights (depending on size) from it. If you have a large lot, you may want to have a second garden transformer on the front side of the house, perhaps smaller for two or three lights. Avoid using doorbell transformers; most of them are made only for intermittent use.

Try to install each transformer at some central location, so two or more short cords can run from it to your lights, rather than one lengthy cord (there is more line-loss of current at 12 volts than at 120 volts). With the two-wire No. 12 cord generally used on low-voltage garden lighting, a run should not exceed 100 feet. If it needs to be longer than 100 feet, use a heavier cord.

You can install a transformer several ways. The simplest is to obtain one with a weatherproof case and plug-in cord, and just plug to a convenient outlet on the patio, house exterior, or in the garage—as if it were a lamp.

If the outlet you choose is not controlled by a switch inside the house, you can use a transformer with a built-in switch. But this means that you will have to step outdoors to turn the lights on and off at the transformer, so it is usually better to rewire that outlet for a switch indoors. If you are not familiar with house wiring, have an electrician do this small job. He may run 120-volt wiring back indoors to a switch. Or he may place a l-v switching relay at the outlet, and run doorbell wiring back to a convenient switch.

There is still another answer to an unswitched outlet: automatic switching. You can buy l-v garden-light transformers with built-in timers that automatically turn the garden lights on and off at any desired hours each evening. Or you can include a photo-electric switch at the outlet that will turn the lights on at sundown and off at dawn. With either,

*SIX LAMPS dramatize small garden at end of carport. Light creates shadows from magnolia and acanthus, right. It silhouettes foreground rocks, nandina, Japanese maple, center; emphasizes plants lit from below.*

the efficient l-v lights use so little current that the expense of their being on for some additional hours is negligible.

If there is a convenient location inside the house, you can wire in a lower cost transformer. This usually requires a wiring permit; a weatherproof garden transformer with a plug-in cord does not. When you first install a 100-watt transformer, it may produce a noticeable hum. After a few weeks, it "wears in" and the hum disappears or greatly diminishes.

The 12-volt cables running from the transformer to your garden lights are usually a "zipcord" type, similar in appearance to the cord for an electric toaster, only slightly heavier (two #12 wires) and with more weatherproof insulation.

You can simply bury these cords in the ground—in fact, it is best, as they then are protected from the sun. Place them 6 inches deep where possible, and try to run them alongside walks, fences, planter-bed edgings, and water lines, so you will not dig them up when cultivating.

Where a cord needs to cross a lawn, simply cut a slit-type trench, wedging it open with your shovel. Push the wire into it and then tamp the turf back in place.

You can connect your garden lights along the main cords, or you can run stub lines to different fixtures. The latter is preferable when you wish to

install a fixture up on a fence or above an entry-way, because you do not need to run the stub line farther to other lights, and it can be a small cord, even the #18 zipcord used on table lamps. You can hide this cord quite easily along wood and masonry joints, and along moldings.

For a fixture in a tree, just staple a cord up the back side of the trunk. Attach it loosely to allow for the tree's growth.

You can connect a stub line to a main cord with soldered joints, or screw-on or crimp-on connectors. With the latter two, coat the finished connections with any rubber seam compound—not for shock protection, but to prevent fertilizers and the like from corroding the connections.

When you stake a light fixture in the ground, bury at least a foot of slack cord alongside it to provide for future adjustments of the fixture as the plantings around it grow.

Making your own light fixtures from some wood, masonry, ceramic, or metal item on hand is quite simple with one of the l-v sockets. Experiment with the light at night, and then attach it with screws, bolts, or epoxy glue.

Very adaptable for l-v light fixtures are the small aluminum cans in which some brands of beer are sold. Those rustproof cans can be used to add small lights in dark corners of the garden to supplement your other lights.

## HEATING THE GARDEN

Because the chill of the evening comes too soon in many outdoor living rooms, the inventive Westerner has worked out many heating schemes. All successful devices are based on radiating heat to the people on the patio, rather than on heating the air.

The firepit is the most used device. In making one, don't get it too deep. As soon as the heat source is below the level of the patio floor, it's of no value to those sitting around it. A raised pit is more effective than a sunken one. You are warmed by heat radiated from the walls of the raised pit as well as the fire itself.

The firepit is not as efficient as the old brick or stone outdoor fireplace. The advantage of the pit is that it provides a source for fire that more or less disappears when not in use. But if your outdoor room can take a fireplace unobtrusively, it is a better bet than a firepit. A back wall for an open fire gives the same effect as a fireplace. In the photographs and sketches on this page and the next page are several schemes that have been used.

The reflection and radiation of heat is all-important in garden heating. The half circle of bricks, for example, will radiate heat long after the fire dies

down. If the concrete raised pit were faced with stainless steel, the radiation would be intensified. Evening sitting arrangement would be in front of the fire, of course. The objections raised with firepits of this type are the same as with fireplaces. If they are built to face away from the house, there is no daytime appearance problem. In all cases the sight of the open fire has a warming effect that is greater than the actual heat release. The open fire is important in night lighting, too.

The portable barbecue can be used as a heat source after the cooking is over. Of course, the greater the size of the brazier, the more heat will be radiated. The metal kettle type will keep shins and knees warm for an hour or more.

The warm floor panel, obtained by installing pipe in a concrete slab, or beneath tile or brick in sand, is being used to some extent. A heated floor will make a 55° air temperature feel comfortable if there is no wind and if the patio has an overhead cover. The warm floor is not cheap. A hot-water heater, small pump, and a good hundred feet of pipe are needed.

It's easier to warm a covered patio than one that is open to the sky. Sitting on an open terrace at night, you lose heat to the sky—more to a clear sky, less to

*FIREPIT, SLIGHTLY RAISED*

*RAISED PIT, ONE SIDE OPEN*

*HALF CIRCLE OF BRICKS*

*RAISED PIT AND TABLE*

*QUARTZ-TUBE, INFRA-RED electric heater under roof keeps patio in use year-around for play, relaxation.*

*PORTABLE gas-fired infrared patio heater for use anywhere outdoors, casts 12 to 15-foot circle of heat.*

a cloudy one. You lose heat to moving air in proportion to rate of movement. You lose heat to all nearby surfaces that are colder than you are. With an air temperature of 55°to 60°, the open sky may be equivalent to a ceiling whose temperature is 32° to 39°. Underneath an overhead, the ceiling will be about the same as the air temperature.

Home owners have worked out some ingenious ways to use reflected heat. An overhead reflector cone above the fire is one such method. Others have experimented with aluminum-faced panels, trying to "bounce" the heat so that when you sit before an open fire your back will be warm.

## Portable patio heater

Patio and poolside living can be extended well into the cool months of fall, by using a portable patio heater. Fired by an enclosed 5-gallon tank of propane, it requires no gas or electrical connection and can be moved anywhere you want it and can

be stored away under shelter when you do not need it.

Almost 8 feet tall, the large unit is rated at 50,000 BTUs per hour, as much as a small house furnace. One will operate about 10 hours at full capacity on a 5-gallon propane tank.

As it emits mainly infrared rays, reflecting them downwards and out, it immediately and efficiently warms you, the furniture, and the deck or ground, rather than the outdoor air. However, it does work best in a wind-sheltered area, because then the objects heated by the infrared rays will also warm the surrounding air to some extent. The cost of the heater, including its propane tank, is around $300.

Similar semiportable infrared heaters are available that connect with a hose to a natural gas line or household propane tank. Other models are for permanent installation with rigid piping to a gas line. In both cases the cost is about $200. There is also a 25,000-BTU propane patio heater for about $150, and still smaller campground-patio models for $60.

## COOLING THE GARDEN WITH WATER

Water in motion gives a garden such a fresh breath that it is worth considering in almost any plan, and there are ways to get it at very little cost. In hot, dry climates where soaring temperatures outside tend to keep you inside, water cooling can make a big difference in how you use the garden.

You may think that the sight of a small garden pool or the sound of a sprinkler running makes you feel cooler only because it suggests a mountain pool or waterfall. But it has more than a psychological effect on your physical comfort. A knowledge of the principles of evaporation and radiation will help you to control your garden climate.

### Evaporation

When hot dry air passes over water—on your skin, on the lawn, on the shrubs, on a terrace pavement—the water evaporates. To evaporate the water, the hot air uses up some of its heat, becomes cooler. The drier the air, the lower the humidity and the greater the heat loss through evaporation. This means that when a hot dry breeze moves through water, it becomes a cool breeze. Of course, if the humidity is high, evaporation is slight and the breeze is not cooled perceptibly.

But wherever humidity is low, you can reduce the temperature in your garden room by getting water into the air. Even a garden sprinkler will do this, but at the cost of very soggy ground and drenched surfaces.

For installations in a garden cooling system, look for spray heads that make a fine mist. There are many on the market, but they are not generally available at nurseries and garden stores. If your nurseryman won't order them for you, check with commercial growers. They use mist sprays in propagating beds, in greenhouses, and in shade houses.

There are several types of spray heads. They are available in various nozzle sizes. Some throw such a fine fog that they use only 3 gallons of water an hour. Look around your garden for places to use the mist sprays and foggers. They use so little water that they can be operated constantly without creating drainage problems. Vine-covered pergolas offer opportunities. For most efficient cooling, keep the vine

*GARDEN POOL illustrates interesting use of irregular shaped design to contrast with plants of various leaf form and texture. Pool is of simple construction, adds a note of interest to garden.*

damp on the windward side. For double-duty, install a mist spray over moisture-loving plants in a lath shelter. Both you and your plants will love it!

*Note:* One of the main objections to mist sprays has been the likelihood of overwatering when operation is continuous. This objection can be overcome by adding automatic timers to the installation.

## Radiation

A hot object, surrounded by cold objects, loses heat to the cold objects. If the pavement under your feet is cooler than you are, you lose some of your heat to it. If the garden wall, or the leaves of a vine, are cooler than you are, you feel cooler when you are near them. Thus, to cool yourself, you should cool the objects around you.

This can be as simple as wetting down your patio floor with water, or spraying the fence or vines or trees around you. The longer the surfaces can be kept cool, the longer you will be cool.

One product that is designed for spraying a small quantity of water just where you want it is a small-diameter plastic tube available in lengths of 100 feet. All necessary reducers and couplings are packaged with it. Since the tubing costs but 10 cents a foot, you can carry a fine spray here and there throughout the garden for very little cost. Wind it over canvas roofs, along the fence, under lath, in the shade garden. (You punch the holes, so you get water only where you need it.) Any masonry wall that absorbs water makes an efficient cooling panel when water is being evaporated from its surface.

In every scheme for garden cooling, remember that air temperature is only the measurement of how the thermometer feels. If the air is 90°, you can, with a sprinkling of water, cool the lawn and shrubs and surfaces around you down 10° to 20°, depending on the dryness of the air. With the cool surfaces around you, a 90° air temperature will feel more like 80° or less.

Obviously, no outdoor cooling method will change a 100° day to a 70° day. But when the sun sets and you move within the sight and sound of water that is cooling garden surfaces and the passing breeze, you'll feel much cooler than the thermometer says you should.

*NATIVE PLANT MATERIAL, Japanese maple edge the granite stream bed; there is a waterfall above the pool.*

*VIEW OF POOL shown above reveals rosemary and santolina sheared to round form. Japanese iris in water.*

# Planting for a Purpose

Without a framework of permanent planting—one that is independent of the come and go of petunias, flowering trees, or any seasonal color—your garden can fall apart for weeks or months at a time. In planning a new garden or remodeling an old one, you can avoid this common fault if you establish such a permanent planting framework. Up to a point, in working out your framework, you can look upon plant material and building material as interchangeable. For example:

You can pave with flat-growing plants or with asphalt. You can build walls with shrubs and trees, or wires plus vines, or wood and vines. If you wish to screen a portion of the patio from neighbors or wind you can use panels of wood or canvas or plastic, or a frame supporting a vine or shrub.

If you wish to divide an area with an element that is from 12 to 16 inches high and about as wide, you can build a seat wall of wood, build a low brick wall, or plant a hedge.

There is, however, a world of difference between selecting lumber for fences, walls, trellises, and roofs, and choosing plants for the same purpose. There is some organization in lumber sizes—from 1 by 1-inch to 12 by 12—and they do not change as they grow older. Plants not only increase in size and vary according to the care they receive, but they also vary in their proportions as they grow.

All the plants available to you, however, do divide themselves into definite functional groups. Out of these groups you select the forms needed for your garden frame. You look for the plants in each group that meet these requirements for permanent garden material:

1. Must have good appearance throughout the year, regardless of how its appearance may change with the seasons.

2. Must be well adapted to your climate, exposure, and soil conditions. Temperamental and tender plants should have less important positions, where their loss will not destroy the garden scheme.

From the plants in each group that fulfill these requirements, you can choose those with texture and foliage that are in good relationship to each other and to your garden's background. Selection is not as difficult as it sounds, if you have the courage to build the basic frame with great simplicity. If you fear that simplicity will result in plainness, remember that everything you do with plants of character and structure, or with seasonal color in bulbs, annuals, perennials, roses, or your other favorites, will be more dramatic because of this simple background.

All but the most experienced gardener and designer will achieve more by the use of a few plants than by weaving an intricate tapestry of many.

The green design can give meaning to outdoor space just as walls and furniture do within the house. You should achieve a sense of enclosure, a happy interplay between house structures and garden forms. Each individual tree, shrub, or unit of ground covering should be seen for what it is, not confused by what surrounds it.

If the basic framework of green is properly worked out, the addition of color will prove an easy matter. The role color can play will be more satisfying within the well planned green framework. It also will provide unity during the non-blooming periods of the year.

In considering color in the garden you must remember also that there are many shades and gradations of green itself. This should be kept in mind in

*FEBRUARY FLOWERS brighten this hillside garden. Narcissus in foreground, flowering peaches (right) beside landscaped swimming pool. Rocks dot the garden.*

*BROAD MASS of Mexican sedum interrupted by long ribbon of darker tamarix juniper. Oleanders beyond.*

*FOLIAGE TEXTURES, colors sing out in this border. Mexican sedum, blue fescue, santolina in lower section.*

designing your basic framework as well as the texture, the form, and the size of plant materials.

Consider color in relation to the surroundings, intensity of light, interplay with other colors. All these factors and more combine with one another to produce the colors you see in the flowers and the background.

In general, colors which are next to one another on the spectrum can be made to work together to produce a pleasing harmony. However, we all have personal choices in color, and the combinations should be a joy to your eyes.

Here is a simplified rule to follow when planning garden colors: Place them so that each has a working role with its neighbors—as part of the background, a member of the immediate family, or a prima donna asking for lots of attention.

Masses, solid and dense or light and airy, can be built by interweaving many plants, modulating textures and foliage color, and synchronizing blooms in time and color. But the time to work out such borders is when you know plants so well and see them so clearly as texture and form that you don't need directions for grouping them.

In this discussion we are concerned only with the garden framework—against which you can do as you please, planting nothing, or displaying favorite plants to your heart's content in the many ways suited to your framework.

Remember that the framework is built with blocks, masses, and lines. We are not looking at shrubs, for example, as individuals, but as multiples in a group.

To bring your possible choices of framework material into focus, we have grouped the shrubs, trees, vines, and ground covers by specific function in the garden. We have tried to narrow the field to a few of the very best choices in each classification. For a complete and thorough coverage of Western plants and their uses, see the *Sunset Western Garden Book*.

## Ground covers

The term "ground cover" represents a group of plants of varied habit that are low growing and spreading. They are used primarily to cover unsightly areas of bare soil. The following examples are classed by function.

GREEN CARPETS TO WALK ON—*Anthemis nobilis*, dichondra, Irish moss, Scotch moss, *Mentha requienii*, *Phyla nodiflora*, *Thymus*.

SUBSTANTIAL COVERS FREQUENTLY USED IN LARGE AREAS—*Carissa grandiflora* 'Tuttle', *Ceanothus gloriosus*, *C. griseus horizontalis*, *Euonymus fortunei* (several varieties), *Hedera*, *Juniperus*, *Pachysandra terminalis*, *Pyracantha* 'Walderi', *Vinca minor*.

NOT AS WOODY AS ABOVE, BUT ATTRACTIVE IF PROPERLY CARED FOR—*Ajuga*, *Fragaria chiloensis*, ice plant, *Ophiopogon*.

## Shrubs to 1½ feet

This is a group of woody plants that can be used for low plantings in masses or blocks. Most of these shrubs must be kept low by trimming.

*Berberis buxifolia* 'Nana', *Buxus sempervirens* 'Suffruticosa', *Ceanothus gloriosus*, *Euonymus japonica* 'Microphylla', *Juniperus horizontalis*, *Rosmarinus officinalis* 'Lockwood de Forest' or 'Prostratus', *Trachelospermum jasminoides*.

## Shrubs to 3 feet

This group of shrubs contains some that naturally grow to 3 feet or less and others that must be trimmed to keep them 2 to 3 feet.

*Berberis verruculosa*, *Buxus microphylla japonica*, *Carissa grandiflora* 'Tuttle', *Cotoneaster conspicua* 'Decora', *Daphne odora*, *Hebe buxifolia*, *Juniperus chinensis* 'Pfitzeriana', *Mahonia aquifolium*, *Nandina domestica*, *Pinus mugo mughus*, rhododendrons (some varieties), *Taxus baccata* 'Repandens', *T. cuspidata* 'Nana'.

## Shrubs to 6 feet

This group of plants can provide masses or blocks of foliage to divide space visually: hedges, barriers, backgrounds.

EVERGREENS—NEAT AND DENSE; TRIMMED AND NATURAL—*Aucuba japonica*, *Berberis darwinii*, camellias, *Citrus*, *Ilex cornuta* 'Burfordii', *Pittosporum tobira*.

EVERGREENS—MEDIUM DENSE, FREE GROWING. CAN BE KEPT TO 6 FEET WITHOUT CHANGING THE NATURE OF THE PLANT—*Abelia grandiflora*, *Mahonia aquifolium*, *Nandina domestica*, *Pieris japonica*, *Prunus laurocerasus*.

*TRUE DWARF CITRUS varieties make a solid green divider between court, covered walk in Sunset patio.*

*PANELS with exposed aggregate surface, set between cedar strips. Design: Chaffee-Zumwalt & Associates.*

## Shrubs to 8 feet or more

EVERGREENS TO BE USED FOR PRIVACY, AND FOR SUN AND WIND CONTROL—*Euonymus japonicus, Leptospermum laevigatum, Ligustrum, Myrica californica, Prunus ilicifolia, Pittosporum, Rhamnus alaternus, Taxus cuspidata, Thuja occidentalis, T. plicata,* bamboo, *Podocarpus.*

SHRUBS FOR TALL SCREENS WHERE WIDTH IS NOT A FACTOR—*Arbutus unedo, Escallonia montevidensis, Feijoa sellowiana, Griselinia littoralis,* oleander, *Pyracantha.*

## Arbors, trellises and espaliers

The growth habit of some plants makes it possible to train them as a part of garden structures. Here are a few such plants.

VINES—*Bougainvillea, Cissus, Clematis,* grape, *Hedera, Jasminum officinale, Lonicera hildebrandiana, Trachelospermum jasminoides, Wisteria.*

SHRUBS—*Callistemon viminalis, Camellia sasanqua,* fuchsias, *Grewia, Jasminum nudiflorum, Podocarpus gracilior, Pyracantha,* climbing rose, *Viburnum plicatum.*

## Trees—deciduous and evergreen

HERE ARE TREES TO PROVIDE A CANOPY OF SHADE FOR THE GARDEN OR STREET—*Acer platanoides, Albizia julibrissin, Callistemon citrinus, Celtis australis, Fagus sylvatica, Ficus retusa, Ginkgo biloba, Lagerstroemia, Ligustrum lucidum, Liquidambar styraciflua, Malus, Platanus acerifolia, Podocarpus gracilior, Prunus blireiana, P. caroliniana, Quercus agrifolia, Q. ilex, Zelkova serrata.*

TREES FOR GARDEN AND PATIO—*Acer davidii, Acer palmatum, Albizia julibrissin, Cercis canadensis, Cornus florida, Eucalyptus ficifolia, Hakea laurina, Liquidambar styraciflua, Magnolia grandiflora* 'Majestic Beauty' or 'Samuel Sommer', *Malus, Olea europaea, Pinus, Pistache, Schinus terebinthifolius.*

## Plants that are orderly, neat growers

*Acer palmatum, Aesculus carnea, Aucuba japonica, Camellia japonica, Chamaecyparis obtusa, Cornus florida, Daphne cneorum, Gardenia jasminoides, Itea ilicifolia, Magnolia kobus stellata, Myrsine africana, Osmanthus delavayi, Parrotia persica, Picea glauca* 'Conica', *Pinus mugo mughus, Pittosporum viridiflorum, Quercus rubra, Rhododendron calophytum, Viburnum opulus* 'Nanum'.

*OLEANDERS add a panel of clean dark green foliage above white brick wall along a service entrance. Early summer through fall, plants are covered with white flowers. Invaluable plants for hot, dry areas.*

WHITE CARPET: *sweet alyssum ground cover accents bottle brushes. On this side of path, lawn, ice plant.*

STAR IVY, *a small-leafed type, grows on wires to screen windows from drive. Design: Armstrong & Sharfman.*

SMALL-LEAFED IVIES *trained on wire-covered fence. Screens driveway, and the service area from the garden.*

'EUREKA' LEMON FENCE *at Sunset. Dwarf varieties are especially well adapted to this kind of use.*

*PLANTS ARE TRANSFORMED by night lighting. Here one lamp is beyond translucent gate, one set in planter, four in the ground. All of the fixtures used in this photo were the low voltage type.*

### Plants that are slow-growing

TREES—*Acer campestre, Amelanchier laevis, Cedrus libani, Ceratonia siliqua, Citrus, Fagus sylvatica, Ginkgo biloba, Liquidambar, Maytenus boaria, Olea europaea, Pinus aristata, Podocarpus falcatus, Prunus subhirtella autumnalis, Taxus baccata.*

SHRUBS—*Arbutus unedo,* azaleas, *Berberis darwinii, Buxus, Cotinus coggygria, Euonymus alata, Ilex crenata* 'Helleri,' *Jasminum sambac, Pieris japonica, Raphiolepis indica, Skimmia japonica, Tsuga canadensis* 'Pendula'.

### Plants that are rugged

*Acacia armata, Acacia pycnantha, Arbutus menziesii, Arctostaphylos manzanita, Buddleia davidii, Carissa grandiflora* 'Fancy', *Ceanothus, Cotoneaster lactea, Cupressocyparis leylandii, Elaeagnus angustifolia, Escallonia montevidensis, Eucalyptus sideroxylon, Forsythia suspensa, Fremontodendron californicum, Lonicera nitida, Mahonia aquifolium, Nerium oleander, Pinus contorta, Platanus racemosa, Pyracantha coccinea, Romneya coulteri, Schinus molle, Tetrapanax papyriferus, Xylosma congestum.*

### Plants with interesting branch structure

*Acanthus mollis, Acer circinatum, Acer palmatum, Agave, Aralia spinosa,* bamboo, *Catalpa, Chaenomeles, Dodonaea viscosa, Enkianthus campanulatus, Fagus sylvatica, Lagerstroemia indica, Larix decidua, Magnolia denudata, Nyssa sylvatica, Pinus thunbergiana, Podocarpus totara, Quercus palustris, Salix babylonica, Sequoia sempervirens.*

### Plants to grow under low windows

*Ajuga reptans, Agapanthus africanus* 'Peter Pan', azalea 'Gumpo', *Bougainvillea* 'Temple Fire', *Bergenia, Ceanothus gloriosus, Convolvulus cneorum, Daphne odora, Echeveria, Hebe buxifolia, Juniperus horizontalis, Mahonia aquifolium* 'Compacta', *Nandina domestica* 'Nana', *Sedum, Taxus baccata* 'Repandens'.

### Plants to grow under high windows

*Aucuba japonica, Azara microphylla, Berberis julianae, Callistemon citrinus, Choisya ternata, Cotoneaster divaricata, Escallonia montevidensis, Feijoa*

*CARMEL CREEPER* (Ceanothus griseus horizontalis) *is best near coast; plant on east or north slopes in hot climates. Chlorotic in highly alkaline soils. Takes wind, salt spray, drought. Here, contrasts with wall.*

*sellowiana, Grewia, Hibiscus rosa-sinensis, Ligustrum japonicum, Juniperus chinensis* 'Mint Julep', *Mahonia lomariifolia, Osmanthus fragrans, Pittosporum tobira, Podocarpus gracilior, Skimmia japonica, Viburnum carlesii, Viburnum tinus.*

### Plants especially adapted to raised beds

*Antirrhinum majus, Arbutus menziesii, Artemisia,* azalea, *Begonia tuberhybrida, Bougainvillea, Camellia japonica, Centaurea cineraria, Cistus, Crassula falcata, Daphne odora, Dianthus, Echeveria,* fuchsias, *Lupinus, Pelargonium peltatum, Phlox drummondii, Primula malacoides,* rhododendrons, *Rosmarinus officinalis, Thunbergia gibsonii, Tulipa, Viola cornuta,* zinnia.

### Plants to look down on from a deck

*Albizia julibrissin, Aralia spinosa, Bougainvillea, Buddleia, Cornus florida, Cotoneaster parneyi, Eucalyptus ficifolia, Euonymus, Fatsia japonica, Ginkgo biloba, Hedera, Hibiscus, Magnolia grandiflora, Pittosporum tobira,* succulents.

### Plants for night lighting

TREES—*Acer negundo, Betula, Cedrus deodara, Eucalyptus cinerea, Fagus sylvatica, Liquidambar styraciflua, Olea europaea, Pinus contorta, Platanus, Podocarpus, Populus alba, Quercus garryana, Sorbus aucuparia.*

SHRUBS—*Acacia, Acer palmatum,* azalea, camellias, *Cordyline australis, Fatsia japonica, Ficus elastica* 'Decora', *Lagerstroemia indica, Mahonia lomariifolia, Nandina domestica, Tetrapanax papyriferus, Yucca aloifolia.*

OTHERS—*Agapanthus, Agave,* bamboo, *Cycas revoluta,* ferns, *Kalanchoe laciniata, Phoenix roebelenii, Sedum, Senecio cineraria, Trachycarpus fortunei.*

### Plants to cascade over a wall

*Arctostaphylos, Asparagus sprengeri, Beaumontia grandiflora, Bougainvillea, Carissa, Ceanothus griseus horizontalis, Cistus hybridus, Cotoneaster dammeri, Daphne cneorum,* fuchsia, *Hedera, Jasminum mesnyi, Juniperus conferta, Lantana, Lonicera, Lotus berthelotii, Mahernia verticillata, Polygonum aubertii, Thunbergia gibsonii, Trachelospermum jasminoides, Vinca minor, Wisteria.*

FENCE *makes rustic background for bank of rhododendrons. Design: Arthur W. Erfeldt & Associate.*

DRAMATIC DISPLAY *outside bedroom glass wall: Hawaiian tree fern. Design: Wimmer and Yamada.*

SCREEN PLANTING *of* Hakea suaveolens *at top of a bank. It looks very much like a conifer.*

SUNNY CARPET: *Orange gazania ground cover sets off* Pittosporum tobira *(left), and the pine.*

WATERFALL in a Japanese garden. Natural rock setting provides perfect background for masses of ferns.

FERN ASPARAGUS, hardy, bugless, thrives in sun or shade. Any soil, if well drained; average water.

LUXURIANT MASS of unusual foliage patterns grows beneath tree. Hosta, bleeding heart, Lenten rose.

CREEPING ROSEMARY, very effective against rock wall. Needs full sun, fast drainage, and little water.

FLOWERY CASCADES—*Alyssum saxatile, Arabis, Campanula isophylla, Gazania, Iberis, Lobelia, Pelargonium peltatum, Petunia hybrida, Phlox subulata, Tropaeolum majus, Verbena peruviana, Zauschneria.*

## Plants for hillsides

SHRUBS—*Acacia longifolia, Carissa grandiflora* 'Prostrata', *Ceanothus gloriosus, Cistus, Cotoneaster* (low growing kinds), *Forsythia, Juniperus* (low growing kinds), *Mahonia repens, Pyracantha* 'Santa Cruz', *Rosa banksiae, Rosmarinus officinalis, Taxus baccata* 'Repandens', *Xylosma congestum.*

PERENNIALS—*Ajuga reptans, Bergenia,* ferns (native), *Fragaria chiloensis, Gazania* (trailing), *Lotus berthelotii, Phyla nodiflora, Verbena, Vinca, Zauschneria.*

VINES—*Bougainvillea, Euonymus fortunei* 'Azusa', *Hedera, Lonicera henryi, Passiflora jamesonii, Tecomaria capensis, Trachelospermum jasminoides.*

GRASSES—Bamboos (low growing kinds), Bermuda (hybrid), *Cortaderia selloana, Zoysia tenuifolia.*

SUCCULENTS—Ice plants (several kinds, including: *Carpobrotus, Cephalophyllum, Delosperma, Dorotheanthus, Drosanthemum, Lampranthus, Mesembryanthemum, Oscularia*), *Sedum.*

## Plants for shady entries and overhangs

GROUND COVERS (UNDER ONE FOOT) FOR ATTRACTIVE FOLIAGE PATTERN—*Asparagus falcatus, Hedera, Pachysandra terminalis, Rhoicissus capensis, Soleirolia soleirolii.*

GROUND COVERS (UNDER ONE FOOT) FOR FLOWERS OR FRUITS—*Ardisia japonica, Asparagus sprengeri, Epimedium grandiflorum, Erythronium, Linnaea borealis, Primula obconica, Ramonda myconi, Skimmia reevesiana, Vinca, Viola odorata.*

PLANTS FROM 1-3 FEET HIGH FOR ATTRACTIVE FOLIAGE PATTERN—*Aspidistra elatior, Caladium,* fern (many hardy and tropical kinds), *Hosta.*

PLANTS FROM 1-3 FEET HIGH FOR FLOWERS AND FRUITS—*Acanthus mollis, Bergenia, Clivia, Helleborus, Impatiens, Rehmannia angulata, Sarcococca humilis, Sollya fusiformis, Tradescantia virginiana, Trillium, Vancouveria.*

BACKGROUND PLANTS (3-6 FEET OR MORE) FOR ATTRACTIVE FOLIAGE PATTERN—*Acer circinatum, Fatsia japonica, Ficus elastica, Griselinia lucida, Howeia, Hydrangea anomala petiolaris, Podocarpus, Rhapis,* tree ferns.

BACKGROUND PLANTS (3-6 FEET OR MORE) FOR FLOWERS OR FRUITS—*Aucuba japonica,* fuchsias, *Hoya, Mahonia, Osmanthus, Skimmia japonica, Tetrapanax papyriferus, Umbellularia californica.*

*FEATHERY FOLIAGE and dense habit make tamarix juniper a favorite ground cover shrub. Junipers are tough, hardy, drought-resistant, widely available, and relatively free from disease, insects. Many varieties.*

GRAY-LEAFED Calocephalus brownii, *yellow-flowered Hottentot fig mingle on this bank near the beach.*

WEEPING DEODAR (Cedrus deodara 'Pendula') *displays itself against gray boulder. Design: George Schenk.*

MOSS PINKS (Phlox subulata) *hold their own against carpet of miniature sedum. Gray boulders contrast.*

VARIEGATED TOBIRA. *Creamy green; sun or shade. In full sun, plants grow into compact, informal hedge.*

FORM AND COLOR *of 8-foot-tall juniper (Juniperus chinensis 'Torulosa') displayed against light brick wall.*

FIERY RED *flower brushes of lemon bottle brush bloom in May and well into summer.*

TAMARIX JUNIPER AND NANDINA *combine effectively with bamboo stake fence and stones.*

CALIFORNIA PEPPER TREE *casts filtered shade throughout the year. Prickly pear grows in foreground.*

## Plants to screen out a noisy road

*Acacia cyclops, Acacia farnesiana, Acacia melanoxylon, Arbutus unedo, Bambusa oldhami, Cedrus deodara, Elaeagnus pungens, Eucalyptus robusta, Eucalyptus stellulata, Ilex aquifolium, Juniperus virginiana, Ligustrum japonicum, Nerium oleander, Pittosporum tobira, Pyracantha, Populus alba* 'Pyramidalis', *Rhus ovata, Schinus molle, Sequoia sempervirens, Taxus, Thuja plicata, Viburnum tinus.*

## Windbreaks

*Acacia cyclops, Acacia melanoxylon, Bambusa oldhami, Calocedrus decurrens, Cupressus macrocarpa, Escallonia, Eucalyptus cladocalyx, E. gunnii, E. robusta, E. spathulata, Juniperus scopulorum, Ligustrum japonicum* 'Texanum', *Lonicera tatarica, Pinus canariensis, Pinus nigra, Pittosporum crassifolium, Populus nigra* 'Italica', *Prunus lyonii, Pyracantha* (tall growing), *Taxus baccata* 'Stricta', *Thuja occidentalis.*

## Plants for narrow beds

IN SUN—*Aeonium, Aster dumosus, Citrus, Daphne cneorum, Erica carnea, Hemerocallis, Iris, Lavandula spica, Moraea iridioides, Pinus mugo mughus, Pittosporum phillyraeoides, Sedum.*

IN SHADE—*Asparagus* (ornamental), *Aspidistra elatior, Bergenia, Camellia sasanqua, Clivia miniata, Cordyline stricta, Impatiens,* ferns, *Hedera helix, Pachysandra terminalis, Sarcococca ruscifolia, Viburnum davidii, Zantedeschia.*

IN SUN OR SHADE—*Agapanthus africanus,* azaleas (Macrantha), *Gardenia jasminoides, Hypericum calycinum, Ilex crenata, Juniperus* (upright forms), *Lobelia, Mahonia, Petunia hybrida, Phylostachys, Ternstroemia gymnanthera, Trachelospermum jasminoides, Tropaeolum.*

## Plants that are easy to grow

SHRUBS—*Arbutus unedo, Aucuba, Callistemon citrinus, Chaenomeles, Feijoa sellowiana, Ligustrum japonicum, Myrtus communis* 'Compacta', *Nerium oleander, Podocarpus gracilior, Raphiolepis indica, Sarcococca, Xylosma congestum.*

PERENNIALS—*Agapanthus africanus, Hemerocallis, Iris* (tall bearded).

ANNUALS—*Begonia semperflorens, Lobularia maritima, Petunia hybrida, Tagetes.*

VINES—*Hedera canariensis, Hedera helix, Parthenocissus, Trachelospermum jasminoides.*

NATIVES—*Acer circinatum, Arctostaphylos columbiana, Arctostaphylos hookeri, Ceanothus gloriosus, Gaultheria shallon, Holodiscus discolor, Mahonia aquifolium, Myrica californica, Prunus ilicifolia, Rhus glabra, Ribes sanguineum, Vaccinium ovatum.*

## Summer color in the shade

Bedding begonias (white, pink, rose or red), tuberous begonias, *Campanula isophylla* (white), *Beloperone guttata* (shrimp and chartreuse), *Francoa ramosa* (white), fuchsias, *Impatiens* (white, orange, pink, or shades of red), *Hydrangea* (white, pink or

*DWARF CHINESE HOLLY. Shiny, deep green leaves; no berries. Will fill in to form a low hedge.*

*CARPET OF AJUGA almost covers stepping stones on path. Contrast in texture makes for added interest.*

blue), *Hosta* (white or lavender), Jacobinia carnea (pink to rose), *Mimulus tigrinus* (yellow with maroon and brown spots), *Primula obconica* (white, pink, lavender or reddish purple).

## Plants with gray foliage

Low (TO 1 FOOT)—*Achillea clavennae argentea, Alyssum saxatile, Artemisia schmidtiana 'Nana', Centaurea cineraria, Cerastium tomentosum, Euphorbia myrsinites, Sedum brevifolium, Sempervivum arachnoideum, Thymus lanuginosus.*

MEDIUM HEIGHT (1-3 FEET)—*Artemisia albula 'Silver Queen', Centaurea gymnocarpa, Dianthus caryophyllus, Lotus berthelotii, Nepeta mussinii, Salvia officinalis, Senecio cineraria, Zauschneria californica.*

TALL (3 FEET AND OVER)—*Artichoke, Cytisus battandieri, Eriogonum arborescens, Lavandula spica, Phlomis fruticosa, Senecio greyii, Teucrium fruticans.*

## Ten dependable annuals for winter-spring color

STOCK—Long, spiky, fragrant, white flowers.

CALENDULA—Daisy-like blossoms in many lovely shades. Good, long lasting cut flowers.

VIOLA (PANSY)—Dancing faces in a rainbow of lovely colors.

BACHELOR BUTTON—Tall and branching. Many colors—the blue is the favorite boutonniere.

CLARKIA—Attractive in mixed borders or alone in mass displays.

CALIFORNIA POPPY—Nodding heads of golden yellow. Good naturalized.

*GOLDEN BAMBOO screen softens wall separating family room deck from patio. To keep graceful, thin out.*

SWEET PEAS—Fragrant blooms to train on a trellis; or plant the new bush variety.

FORGET-ME-NOT—Tiny, clear-blue, white centered flowers; long blooming season.

SNAPDRAGON—Saucy spikes in many colors. There are good new dwarf varieties.

SWEET ALYSSUM—Tiny white flowers crowded into clusters; honey-like fragrance. Useful as a border or a carpet.

## Ten dependable annuals for summer color

ZINNIA—Long-time garden favorite; colorful hot weather plants.

MARIGOLD—Robust, nearly trouble-free plants ranging from 6 inches to 4 feet. Flowers from pale yellow through gold to orange and brown-maroon.

PETUNIA—Popular bedding plant, single to very double, many colors.

NASTURTIUM—Easy culture, rapid growth; climbing or compact. Colors range through maroon, red-brown, orange, yellow and red to creamy white.

DIANTHUS—Many varieties in single or double form. Thrive in full sun. White, shades of pink, rose, red, yellow and orange.

AGERATUM—Reliable favorite for color in borders or containers. Tiny lavender-blue, white or pink flowers in dense tassel-like clusters.

IMPATIENS—Erect and branching plant. Flowers are large and spurred, colors plain or variegated in white, pink, rose, lilac, and red.

DAHLIA—Excellent cut flowers, many colors, dwarf or tall. Can lift and store tubers.

CHINA ASTER—Splendid cut flower and effective bedding plant. Many different flower forms in a wide range of colors.

COSMOS—Showy daisylike flowers in many colors and forms.

## Three bulb favorites for accents of color

There are many bulbs that can be used for bright splashes of color in your garden. Here we have chosen only the favorites, but there are many more.

NARCISSUS—Valuable spring flowering plants. Permanent and hardy. Colors basically yellow and white but with variations.

TULIP—Best in cold winter climates, but can be grown elsewhere. Some are stately; others dainty; a few bizarre. Many uses—garden, containers, and for cutting. Tulips are spring flowering.

IRIS—Large, diverse group of plants;varying flower form and color, cultural needs and blooming season. Choose those to fit your needs. The majority of these lovely plants bloom in spring or early summer.

*CALIFORNIA POPPIES, sown in November, photographed in April, provide erosion control on this slope until permanent plants, including pines, become established. Raw bank becomes attractive.*

*PRIMROSE PATH is an April delight. Plants are grouped by color: white, cream, yellow, terra-cotta red, blue, lavender, pink. Seeds sown annually for continuous supply of new plants. Design: William Cole.*

# PHOTOGRAPHERS

COVER PHOTOGRAPH BY ROBERT COX

JERRY ANSON: page 47 top left. WILLIAM APLIN: pages 41, 42 top right, 42 bottom right, 44, 49, 58, 59, 70 bottom left, 71 bottom left, 134 right, 135 left, 143 left, 144, 149 top right, 152 bottom left, 155 bottom right, 156 top left, 156 bottom, 157 left, 159 top. APLIN-DUDLEY STUDIOS: page 47 bottom right. MORLEY BAER: pages 30 top left, 30 top right, 104. JEREMIAH O. BRAGSTAD: page 68 bottom right. ERNEST BRAUN: pages 7 top, 28 top right, 29 top left, 29 top right, 55, 78, 80, 81, 121. TOM BURNS: pages 6 top, 42 bottom left. CLYDE CHILDRESS: pages 43 top, 139, 150. GLENN CHRISTIANSEN: pages 52 top, 53, 69, 70 top left, 70 bottom right, 76 top left, 79 bottom right, 141 top, 143 right, 148 bottom, 149 top left, 151, 152 bottom right, 153 top right. NANCY DAVIDSON: pages 68 top, 153 bottom right, 159 bottom. LYN DAVIS: pages 110, 111, 114 bottom right, 115 top left. RICHARD DAWSON: pages 52 bottom left, 155 top left. DEARBORN-MASSAR: pages 105, 127 left. MAX ECKERT: page 61 bottom. RICHARD FISH: pages 31, 32 top right, 42 top left, 66 top left, 66 bottom left, 67 top, 67 bottom right, 76, 82, 83, 94, 95, 100, 101 top, 101 bottom right, 102, 106, 108, 109, 122 left, 133, 134 left. AARON D. FREEMAN: page 32 top left. FRANK L. GAYNOR: page 123 left. WALTER HOUK: page 70 top right. GLEN HUNT: pages 60 top left, 93 top right. ART HUPY: pages 98 top, 98 bottom left, 124 right. ROY KRELL: pages 43 bottom, 61 top right, 132 left, 152 top right. GEORGE LYONS: page 32 bottom left. ELLS MARUGG: pages 48, 79 top, 149 bottom right. DON NORMARK: pages 34, 36, 37, 38, 54, 56, 60 bottom left, 62 top, 63, 64 top, 65, 68 bottom left, 74, 75, 76 top right, 84, 86, 87, 91, 92 top, 97 top right, 97 bottom, 112, 113, 114 top right, 114 bottom left, 115 top right, 116, 127 right, 131, 132 right, 147 right, 152 top left, 153 bottom left, 155 top right, 155 bottom left, 156 top right, 158. PHIL PALMER: pages 33, 77 bottom, 90. RONDAL PARTRIDGE: page 7 bottom. MARION PATTERSON: page 154. TOM RILEY: page 142. JOHN ROBINSON: page 46 bottom right. MARTHA ROSMAN: pages 30 bottom left, 30 bottom right. JULIUS SHULMAN: page 32 bottom right. BLAIR STAPP: page 125. DARROW M. WATT: pages 29 bottom left, 29 bottom right, 39, 40, 71 top, 71 bottom right, 99 top right, 99 bottom, 118, 119, 120, 122 right, 135 right, 136, 137, 146, 147 left, 153 top left. RAY O. WELCH: pages 88 top, 88 bottom left, 89, 93 top left, 93 bottom. MASON WEYMOUTH: pages 123 right, 124 left. STEVE C. WILSON: pages 50, 51, 115 bottom right. GEORGE WOO: pages 4, 72, 73, 115 bottom left.